T0143680

Printed in the USA
CPSIA information can be obtained
at www.ICGtesting.com
JSHW052019140824
68134JS00027B/2552

9 780874 419467

Hineni Express

The *FAST TRACK* to Hebrew and Prayer

BEHRMAN HOUSE
www.behrmanhouse.com

Visit **www.behrmanhouse.com/hineni-express** for further resources.

Designer: Zatar Creative
Project Editor: Ann D. Koffsky
Copyright © 2016 Behrman House, Inc.
Springfield, NJ 07081

ISBN 978-0-87441-946-7

Printed in the United States of America

The publisher gratefully acknowledges the following sources of photographs and images:

Photo credits Hineni Express
The publisher gratefully acknowledges the following sources of photographs:
(T=top, B=bottom, M=middle, L=left, R=right)

Cover and back cover: Behrman House.

Interior: Shutterstock: davooda 4,5, 15 (prayer, from the text, vocabulary icons), Zatar Creative 5 (building blocks icon), Liudmyla Marykon15 (prayer in motion icon), Fine Art 19 (name tag icon), luerat satichob 18 (roots icon), VoodooDot 18, 47 (where we are, prayer variations icons), noppop 5, R. Roth 7, 15, Gregory Gerber 8, tomertu 9, 13, 36M, 36B, 40, Karaidel 11L, 11M, Africa Studio, 11R, 30T, 61, Palakorn Limsatitpong 13, file404 16T, Sergey Nivens 16M, Longjourneys 16B, Cameramannz 19, Arkady Mazor 20, x4wiz 21, Korpithas 22, cubart 23, imging 23, Zita 24, PHOTOCREO Michal Bednarek 25, Champion studio 27, mikhail h 30B, Michel Borges 33, bikeriderlondon 32, bahri altay 34, Kyrylo Glivin35BL, Howard Sandler 35M, Noam Armonn 35R, auremar 30, Robert Hoetink 42, egg design 44, kstudija 45, Bohbeh 47, martin bowra 49, Sappasit 52, AstroStar 53, MANDY GODBEHEAR 54, photomaster 55, Purino 57, Roman Samborskyi 59, michaeljung 60, kanusommer 64, Sean Pavone 68, alexvav 72, Oleg Ivanov IL 76, alexkoral 77, Oleg Zaslavsky78L, blueeyes 78R, Opachevsky Irina 79L, Lemon Tree Images 79R, beeboys 80, photka 81, India Picture 82, irisphoto1 83, sevenke 84, Antonov Roman 87, Kletr 88, Viktorija Reuta 91, SpeedKingz 92. Other sources: Behrman House: 12, 17T, 26, 67, 70M, 75, 79M 85; Rinat Gilboa 50,63; Wikimedia commons: Yeshiva University Museum 28; istock: grahamandgraham 70.

Contents

In our tradition, we say thank you to God for many different things, with prayers called בְּרָכוֹת. Most בְּרָכוֹת begin with the following blessing formula:

$$\text{בָּרוּךְ אַתָּה, יְיָ אֱלֹהֵינוּ, מֶלֶךְ הָעוֹלָם...}$$

Praised are You, Adonai our God, Ruler of the world...

Put a check next to the lines in each blessing below that have these same words.

THINK ABOUT IT!

Why do you think so many blessings begin the same way?

_____

_____

📖 PRAYER

Practice reading these בְּרָכוֹת aloud:

Praised are You, Adonai our God,	בָּרוּךְ אַתָּה, יְיָ אֱלֹהֵינוּ, 1
Ruler of the world,	מֶלֶךְ הָעוֹלָם, 2
who creates	בּוֹרֵא 3
the fruit of the earth (vegetables).	פְּרִי הָאֲדָמָה. 4
Praised are You, Adonai our God,	בָּרוּךְ אַתָּה, יְיָ אֱלֹהֵינוּ, 5
Ruler of the world,	מֶלֶךְ הָעוֹלָם, 6
who creates different kinds of foods.	בּוֹרֵא מִינֵי מְזוֹנוֹת. 7

PRAYER DICTIONARY

בָּרוּךְ
praised, blessed

אַתָּה
you

יְיָ
Adonai

אֱלֹהֵינוּ
our God

מֶלֶךְ
ruler

הָעוֹלָם
the world

בּוֹרֵא
who creates

פְּרִי
(the) fruit (of)

הָאֲדָמָה
the earth

שֶׁהֶחֱיָנוּ
who has given us life

שֶׁהֶחֱיָנוּ

The blessing we say when we are thankful for something new is called the שֶׁהֶחֱיָנוּ. We say it for firsts, like when we wear new clothing for the first time, eat a new fruit that is in season, or celebrate the first night of almost every holiday.

PRAYER
Practice reading the שֶׁהֶחֱיָנוּ:

Praised are You, Adonai our God,	1 בָּרוּךְ אַתָּה, יְיָ אֱלֹהֵינוּ,
Ruler of the world,	2 מֶלֶךְ הָעוֹלָם,
who has given us life, sustained us,	3 שֶׁהֶחֱיָנוּ וְקִיְּמָנוּ
and enabled us to reach this time.	4 וְהִגִּיעָנוּ לַזְּמַן הַזֶּה.

Name a holiday or special occasion when you would say the שֶׁהֶחֱיָנוּ:

_____

FROM THE TEXT
The Talmud teaches that we should say at least 100 בְּרָכוֹת each day. That's a lot! If you were to say 100 blessings in one day, how do you think you might feel that day?

_____

_____

PRAYER BUILDING BLOCKS
בָּרוּךְ "blessed" or "praised."

Most Hebrew words are built on roots. A root usually has three letters. בָּרוּךְ shares a common root—ברכ—with the Hebrew word בֶּרֶךְ, "knee." בָּרוּךְ reminds us that when we say a בְּרָכָה it is as if we are kneeling before Adonai, our Ruler.

Circle the root letters ברכ in these words:

בָּרוּךְ   בֶּרֶךְ   בְּרָכָה

בְּרָכוֹת שֶׁל שַׁבָּת

When guests come to your house, do you greet them at the door? When they leave, do you thank them for coming? We do the same with Shabbat: We welcome and say goodbye to it with blessings. A blessing said before we carry out a commandment is called a בְּרָכָה שֶׁל מִצְוָה. Each begins with the following ten words:

בָּרוּךְ אַתָּה, יְיָ אֱלֹהֵינוּ, מֶלֶךְ הָעוֹלָם,
אֲשֶׁר קִדְּשָׁנוּ בְּמִצְוֹתָיו וְצִוָּנוּ...

**Praised are You, Adonai our God, Ruler of the world,
who makes us holy with God's commandments and commands us...**

We begin Shabbat by lighting candles, saying the קִדּוּשׁ, and eating hallah.

PRAYER

Practice reading these בְּרָכוֹת aloud:

Praised are You, Adonai our God,	בָּרוּךְ אַתָּה, יְיָ אֱלֹהֵינוּ,	1
Ruler of the world,	מֶלֶךְ הָעוֹלָם,	2
who makes us holy	אֲשֶׁר קִדְּשָׁנוּ	3
with commandments and commands us	בְּמִצְוֹתָיו וְצִוָּנוּ	4
to light the Sabbath light (candles).	לְהַדְלִיק נֵר שֶׁל שַׁבָּת.	5
Praised are You, Adonai our God,	בָּרוּךְ אַתָּה, יְיָ אֱלֹהֵינוּ,	6
Ruler of the world,	מֶלֶךְ הָעוֹלָם,	7
who creates the fruit of the vine.	בּוֹרֵא פְּרִי הַגָּפֶן.	8
Praised are You, Adonai our God,	בָּרוּךְ אַתָּה, יְיָ אֱלֹהֵינוּ,	9
Ruler of the world,	מֶלֶךְ הָעוֹלָם,	10
who brings forth bread	הַמּוֹצִיא לֶחֶם	11
from the earth.	מִן הָאָרֶץ.	12

PRAYER DICTIONARY

אֲשֶׁר
who

קִדְּשָׁנוּ
makes us holy

בְּמִצְוֹתָיו
with God's commandments

וְצִוָּנוּ
and commands us

לְהַדְלִיק
to light

נֵר
a light, candle

שֶׁל
of

שַׁבָּת
Shabbat

PRAYER DICTIONARY

הַגָּפֶן
the vine

הַמּוֹצִיא
who brings forth

לֶחֶם
bread

מִן
from

הָאָרֶץ
the earth

 PRAYER

We mark the end of Shabbat by reciting havdalah, which includes the blessing over wine and these three בְּרָכוֹת below:

1 בָּרוּךְ אַתָּה, יְיָ אֱלֹהֵינוּ, ... *Praised are You, Adonai our God,*

2 מֶלֶךְ הָעוֹלָם, ... *Ruler of the world,*

3 בּוֹרֵא מִינֵי בְשָׂמִים. .... *who creates the varieties of spices.*

4 בָּרוּךְ אַתָּה, יְיָ אֱלֹהֵינוּ, ... *Praised are You, Adonai our God,*

5 מֶלֶךְ הָעוֹלָם, ... *Ruler of the world,*

6 בּוֹרֵא מְאוֹרֵי הָאֵשׁ. .... *who creates the fiery lights.*

7 בָּרוּךְ אַתָּה, יְיָ אֱלֹהֵינוּ, ... *Praised are You, Adonai our God,*

8 מֶלֶךְ הָעוֹלָם, ... *Ruler of the world,*

9 הַמַּבְדִיל בֵּין קֹדֶשׁ .... *who separates the holy from*

10 לְחוֹל, בֵּין אוֹר לְחשֶׁךְ, ... *the everyday, light from darkness,*

11 בֵּין יִשְׂרָאֵל לָעַמִּים, ... *Israel from the other nations,*

12 בֵּין יוֹם הַשְּׁבִיעִי .... *the seventh day from*

13 לְשֵׁשֶׁת יְמֵי הַמַּעֲשֶׂה. .... *the six days of work.*

14 בָּרוּךְ אַתָּה יְיָ, ... *Praised are You, Adonai,*

15 הַמַּבְדִיל בֵּין .... *who separates*

16 קֹדֶשׁ לְחוֹל. .... *the holy from the everyday.*

Why do you think there are blessings to mark the beginning and end of Shabbat?

PRAYER BUILDING BLOCKS

קִדְּשָׁנוּ "makes us holy"

קִדְּשָׁנוּ is made up of two parts:
קִדֵּשׁ means "makes holy."
נוּ means "us" or "our."

קִדְּשָׁנוּ is built on the root letters קדש.

The letters קדש tell us that _____ is part of a word's meaning.

בְּמִצְוֹתָיו "with God's commandments"

The Hebrew word for "commandments" is מִצְוֹת.
Circle the part of the word that means "commandments" in בְּמִצְוֹתָיו.

וְצִוָּנוּ means "and commands us"

וְצִוָּנוּ is made up of three parts:
וְ means "and."
צִוָּ means "commands."
נוּ means "us."

The letters צו appear in both of the following words:

וְצִוָּנוּ   בְּמִצְוֹתָיו

Draw a circle around the letters צו in the two words above.

The letters צו let us know that "command" is part of a word's meaning.

בְּרָכוֹת שֶׁל יוֹם טוֹב

Some בְּרָכוֹת שֶׁל מִצְוָה are said before fulfilling a holiday mitzvah, like lighting the menorah.

Put a check next to the בְּרָכוֹת שֶׁל מִצְוָה on pages 9 and 10 that are recited only before a holiday-related mitzvah. *(Hint: Look for the ten words we discussed on page 6.)*

PRAYER

Practice reading these blessings recited on the following occasions:

Rosh Hashanah Blessings

Praised are You, Adonai our God,	בָּרוּךְ אַתָּה, יְיָ אֱלֹהֵינוּ, 1
Ruler of the world,	מֶלֶךְ הָעוֹלָם, 2
who creates the fruit of the tree.	בּוֹרֵא פְּרִי הָעֵץ. 3
Praised are You, Adonai our God,	בָּרוּךְ אַתָּה, יְיָ אֱלֹהֵינוּ, 4
Ruler of the world, who makes us holy	מֶלֶךְ הָעוֹלָם, אֲשֶׁר קִדְּשָׁנוּ 5
with commandments and commands us	בְּמִצְוֺתָיו וְצִוָּנוּ 6
to hear the sound of the shofar.	לִשְׁמֹעַ קוֹל שׁוֹפָר. 7

Sukkot Blessings

Praised are You, Adonai our God,	בָּרוּךְ אַתָּה, יְיָ אֱלֹהֵינוּ, 8
Ruler of the world, who makes us holy	מֶלֶךְ הָעוֹלָם, אֲשֶׁר קִדְּשָׁנוּ 9
with commandments and commands us	בְּמִצְוֺתָיו וְצִוָּנוּ 10
to sit in the sukkah.	לֵישֵׁב בַּסֻּכָּה. 11
Praised are You, Adonai our God,	בָּרוּךְ אַתָּה, יְיָ אֱלֹהֵינוּ, 12
Ruler of the world, who makes us holy	מֶלֶךְ הָעוֹלָם, אֲשֶׁר קִדְּשָׁנוּ 13
with commandments and commands us	בְּמִצְוֺתָיו וְצִוָּנוּ 14
to shake the lulav.	עַל נְטִילַת לוּלָב. 15

בְּרָכוֹת

 **PRAYER**

Practice reading these holiday blessings:

Hanukkah Blessings

Praised are You, Adonai our God,	בָּרוּךְ אַתָּה, יְיָ אֱלֹהֵינוּ,	1
Ruler of the world,	מֶלֶךְ הָעוֹלָם,	2
who makes us holy	אֲשֶׁר קִדְּשָׁנוּ	3
with commandments and commands us	בְּמִצְוֹתָיו וְצִוָּנוּ	4
to light the Hanukkah candles.	לְהַדְלִיק נֵר שֶׁל חֲנֻכָּה.	5
Praised are You, Adonai our God,	בָּרוּךְ אַתָּה, יְיָ אֱלֹהֵינוּ,	6
Ruler of the world, who did	מֶלֶךְ הָעוֹלָם, שֶׁעָשָׂה	7
miracles for our ancestors	נִסִּים לַאֲבוֹתֵינוּ	8
long ago, at this season.	בַּיָּמִים הָהֵם בַּזְּמַן הַזֶּה.	9

Passover Seder Blessings

Praised are You, Adonai our God,	בָּרוּךְ אַתָּה, יְיָ אֱלֹהֵינוּ,	10
Ruler of the world,	מֶלֶךְ הָעוֹלָם,	11
who makes us holy	אֲשֶׁר קִדְּשָׁנוּ	12
with commandments and commands us	בְּמִצְוֹתָיו וְצִוָּנוּ	13
to eat matzah.	עַל אֲכִילַת מַצָּה.	14
Praised are You, Adonai our God,	בָּרוּךְ אַתָּה, יְיָ אֱלֹהֵינוּ,	15
Ruler of the world,	מֶלֶךְ הָעוֹלָם,	16
who makes us holy	אֲשֶׁר קִדְּשָׁנוּ	17
with commandments and commands us	בְּמִצְוֹתָיו וְצִוָּנוּ	18
to eat bitter herbs.	עַל אֲכִילַת מָרוֹר.	19

PRAYER DICTIONARY

עֵץ
tree

שׁוֹפָר
shofar

בַּסֻּכָּה
in the sukkah

לוּלָב
lulav

חֲנֻכָּה
Hanukkah

נִסִּים
miracles

בַּזְּמַן הַזֶּה
at this season,
at this time

אֲכִילַת
eating (of)

מַצָּה
matzah

BUILDING YOUR VOCABULARY

Read each of the Hebrew words below aloud.

Ⓒircle the Hebrew word that means the same as the English.

shofar	שׁוֹפָר	יִשְׂרָאֵל	שְׁמַע
eating (of)	לוּלָב	הָאֲדָמָה	אֲכִילַת
miracles	הָעוֹלָם	נִסִּים	וְצִוָּנוּ
in the sukkah	בַּסֻּכָּה	אַתָּה	לֶחֶם
fruit	מֶלֶךְ	פְּרִי	נֵר
tree	אַתָּה	אֶחָד	עֵץ

COUNT YOUR BLESSINGS

On the first night of many holidays, like Sukkot and Hanukkah, we recite the שֶׁהֶחֱיָנוּ
in addition to the regular holiday blessings.

On the first night of Hanukkah how many blessings do we say when we light the candles?
1, 3, or 5? _____

How many do we say on the second night? 1, 2, or 5?_____

In the בְּרָכוֹת on page 10, there are special blessings for foods we eat on Passover.

Ⓒircle the Hebrew words for the foods we eat on Passover.

Put a check next to the blessings recited over Passover foods.

How many blessings did you check? _____

בְּרָכוֹת

The קִדּוּשׁ serves as a reminder of two important events, the Creation of the world and the Exodus from Egypt. We say it every Shabbat.

We also say the קִדּוּשׁ on many holidays, including Rosh Hashanah, Sukkot, and Passover. The קִדּוּשׁ marks these occasions as different and separate from the everyday. How else can we remind ourselves that Shabbat and other holidays are separate and sacred?

PRAYER

Practice reading the קִדּוּשׁ for Shabbat aloud:

1	בָּרוּךְ אַתָּה, יְיָ אֱלֹהֵינוּ,	Praised are You, Adonai our God,
2	מֶלֶךְ הָעוֹלָם,	Ruler of the world,
3	בּוֹרֵא פְּרִי הַגָּפֶן.	who creates the fruit of the vine.
4	בָּרוּךְ אַתָּה, יְיָ אֱלֹהֵינוּ,	Praised are You, Adonai our God,
5	מֶלֶךְ הָעוֹלָם, אֲשֶׁר קִדְּשָׁנוּ	Ruler of the world, who makes us holy
6	בְּמִצְוֹתָיו וְרָצָה בָנוּ,	with commandments and takes delight in us.
7	וְשַׁבַּת קָדְשׁוֹ	God has made the holy Sabbath
8	בְּאַהֲבָה וּבְרָצוֹן הִנְחִילָנוּ,	our heritage in love and favor,
9	זִכָּרוֹן לְמַעֲשֵׂה בְרֵאשִׁית.	as a memory of the work of Creation.
10	כִּי הוּא יוֹם תְּחִלָּה לְמִקְרָאֵי קֹדֶשׁ,	It is first among our holy days,
11	זֵכֶר לִיצִיאַת מִצְרָיִם.	a memory of the Exodus from Egypt.
12	כִּי בָנוּ בָחַרְתָּ	You chose us
13	וְאוֹתָנוּ קִדַּשְׁתָּ מִכָּל הָעַמִּים,	from all the nations and You made us holy,
14	וְשַׁבַּת קָדְשְׁךָ	You have given us the Sabbath
15	בְּאַהֲבָה וּבְרָצוֹן הִנְחַלְתָּנוּ.	in (with) love and favor as a sacred inheritance.
16	בָּרוּךְ אַתָּה יְיָ,	Praised are You, Adonai,
17	מְקַדֵּשׁ הַשַּׁבָּת.	who makes the Sabbath holy.

קָדוֹשׁ
sanctification

זִכָּרוֹן
memory

(לְ)מַעֲשֵׂה בְּרֵאשִׁית
work of creation

זֵכֶר
memory

(לִ)יצִיאַת מִצְרַיִם
going out from Egypt

בְּאַהֲבָה
in (with) love

וּבְרָצוֹן
and in (with) favor

BUILDING YOUR VOCABULARY

Read the Hebrew words aloud.

Circle the Hebrew word that means the same as the English.

memory	זִכָּרוֹן	וְרָצָה
and in (with) favor	אַהֲבָה	וּבְרָצוֹן
memory	מִצְרַיִם	זֵכֶר
sanctification	קָדוֹשׁ	נֵר שֶׁל שַׁבָּת
work of Creation	בָּרוּךְ	מַעֲשֵׂה בְּרֵאשִׁית
in (with) love	בְּרֵאשִׁית	בְּאַהֲבָה
going out from Egypt	יְצִיאַת מִצְרַיִם	לְעוֹלָם וָעֶד

🌱 ROOTS

Words built on the root קדש have "holy" as part of their meaning.

קִדּוּשׁ means "sanctification" (the act of making something holy).

קִדּוּשׁ helps make שַׁבָּת and other holidays holy.

The following words all appear in the קִדּוּשׁ. (Circle) the three root letters in each word. Read each of the words aloud. (Reminder: In the words below, קָ is read as "koh.")

מְקַדֵּשׁ　קָדְשֶׁךָ　קִדַּשְׁתָּ　קִדֵּשׁ　קָדְשׁוֹ　קָדְשׁוֹ　קִדְּשָׁנוּ

Why do you think there are so many words with the root letters קדש in this blessing?

_____

The Jews are members of a "holy nation"—עַם קָדוֹשׁ.

(Circle) three words below that you think best explain what holiness is. You can also add your own word:

sacred	unusual	rare	Godly	**Your word:**
special	cool	different	revered	
fantastic	sanctified	important	precious	_____

Explain why you circled the words above.

_____

_____

Words built on the root זכר have "remember" as part of their meaning.

זִכָּרוֹן means "memory" or "remembrance."

זֵכֶר also means "memory" or "remembrance."

What steps do you take to remember something important, for example, keeping a promise you've made?

_____

📖 FROM THE TEXT

Shabbat is the fourth of the Ten Commandments:

"Remember the Sabbath day and keep it holy." *(Exodus 20:8)*

זָכוֹר אֶת־יוֹם הַשַּׁבָּת לְקַדְּשׁוֹ.

Underline the word in this selection from Exodus that tells us to remember Shabbat. *(Hint: Look for the root letters* זכר.*)*

Why do you think remembering Shabbat is so important that it is one of the Ten Commandments?

_____

_____

🏃 PRAYER IN MOTION

The קִדּוּשׁ is like a play, with actions and props that are there to remind us that Shabbat is a separate and sacred time. Many congregations and families have a cup that they just use for the קִדּוּשׁ. The cup is filled right to the top for the קִדּוּשׁ so that it's about to spill and overflow. This symbolizes our hope that our lives will overflow with good things.

The קִדּוּשׁ is recited both in synagogue and in the home. In many congregations, everyone stands as the קִדּוּשׁ is recited. The leader holds the קִדּוּשׁ cup high and the congregation joins in singing for part of the blessing. Others follow the tradition of sitting while the קִדּוּשׁ is recited.

Does your congregation stand or sit while the קִדּוּשׁ is recited?

_____

THE MITZVAH OF REMEMBERING

When we say the קִדּוּשׁ we remember two important events. One
of them is the Creation of the world: מַעֲשֵׂה בְּרֵאשִׁית.

מַעֲשֵׂה means "work of."

בְּרֵאשִׁית means "Creation" ("in the beginning").

בְּרֵאשִׁית is also the Hebrew name for Genesis,
the first book of the Torah.

Here is the first verse in the Book of Genesis. Underline the
word בְּרֵאשִׁית.

בְּרֵאשִׁית בָּרָא אֱלֹהִים אֵת הַשָּׁמַיִם וְאֵת הָאָרֶץ.

Why do you think this book of the Torah is called בְּרֵאשִׁית?

_____

The second important event we remember in the קִדּוּשׁ is the Exodus from Egypt,
יְצִיאַת מִצְרַיִם. On which holiday do we celebrate יְצִיאַת מִצְרַיִם?

_____

Why do you think it is so important for us to remember each of these events?

מַעֲשֵׂה בְּרֵאשִׁית

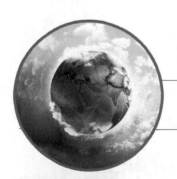

_____

_____

יְצִיאַת מִצְרַיִם

_____

Riiiing! If you hear the bell ring at school, you know class is about to begin. If your teacher dims the lights, it's time to quiet down. What other signals tell you something important is about to start?

The בָּרְכוּ prayer is like those signals—it calls the congregation together and announces that the main part of the prayer service is beginning.

Traditionally we recite the בָּרְכוּ only in the presence of a מִנְיָן—a group of ten or more Jews who are at least of bar or bat mitzvah age. The leader invites the congregation to praise Adonai, and the congregation responds by praising Adonai.

Why do you think this call to prayer is said only when there is a מִנְיָן present?

_____

_____

 PRAYER

Practice reading the בָּרְכוּ aloud:

(The leader chants:)

Praise Adonai, who is to be praised...................... בָּרְכוּ אֶת יְיָ הַמְבֹרָךְ. 1

(The congregation responds:)

Praised is Adonai, who is to be praised.................. בָּרוּךְ יְיָ הַמְבֹרָךְ 2

forever and ever.... לְעוֹלָם וָעֶד. 3

(The leader repeats lines 2 and 3.)

The בָּרְכוּ is also said before the Torah is read. The person honored with the aliyah recites the first line of the בָּרְכוּ and the congregation responds with the second and third line. The person called for the aliyah repeats the second and third line and then recites the blessing before reading from the Torah.

Can you think of other signals that are used more than once? Why do you think signals are sometimes repeated?

ROOTS

Three words in the בָּרְכוּ look and sound similar.

בָּרוּךְ   הַמְבֹרָךְ   בָּרְכוּ

They share the same root letters: ברכ.
(*Reminder:* כּכך *are family letters, so are* בּב.)

(Circle) the three root letters ברכ in each of the above words.

How many times does this root appear in the בָּרְכוּ?

Why do you think words built on this root appear so many times in this prayer?

_____

_____

BUILDING YOUR VOCABULARY

Read each of the Hebrew words aloud.
Then (circle) the Hebrew word(s) corresponding to match the English.

praised, blessed	בָּרוּךְ	לְעוֹלָם וָעֶד אֶת	
forever and ever	אֶת	לְעוֹלָם וָעֶד	בָּרְכוּ
Adonai	יְיָ	בָּרְכוּ	וָעֶד
praise!	אֶת	לְעוֹלָם	בָּרְכוּ
who is to be praised	לְעוֹלָם וָעֶד	הַמְבֹרָךְ	יְיָ

WHERE WE ARE

Look ahead to page 94 and find the בָּרְכוּ in the list of Shabbat morning prayers. On Shabbat morning, the בָּרְכוּ comes right before the _____ blessing.

PRAYER DICTIONARY

בָּרְכוּ
praise!

יְיָ
Adonai

הַמְבֹרָךְ
who is to be praised

בָּרוּךְ
praised, blessed

לְעוֹלָם וָעֶד
forever and ever

GOD'S NAME

God's name is a mystery to us—we don't know how to say it. Since the destruction of the Temple, that knowledge was lost, and we no longer know how God's true name sounds.

Since we don't know how to pronounce it, when we see God's name written as יְיָ or יְהֹוָה, we don't try to read it the way we would other words. Instead, we say אֲדוֹנָי, which means "my Lord."

You may also sometimes see God's name written as 'ה. 'ה is an abbreviation for הַשֵּׁם— The Name. Some people choose to refer to God as הַשֵּׁם rather than אֲדוֹנָי, and will only say אֲדוֹנָי when praying.

WHAT'S IN A NAME?

How did your parents think of your name? Maybe you are named after somebody, or perhaps they thought your name sounded pretty. Prayers get their names in different ways, too. Some are named after their opening words.

Below are the opening phrases from different prayers. (Circle) the name of each of the prayers. (Hint: Look for the first word.) Now read aloud the names of the prayers.

1 וְאָהַבְתָּ אֵת יְיָ אֱלֹהֶיךָ

2 וְשָׁמְרוּ בְנֵי יִשְׂרָאֵל אֶת הַשַּׁבָּת

3 בָּרְכוּ אֶת יְיָ הַמְבֹרָךְ

4 עָלֵינוּ לְשַׁבֵּחַ לַאֲדוֹן הַכֹּל

Other prayers get their name from the main idea of the prayer. Imagine you were writing a new prayer. Would you title it by its opening words, its main idea, or something different? Why?

בָּרְכוּ

FROM THE TEXT

The בָּרְכוּ is very old—it's even older than the siddur itself! Some of its words first appear in the Bible at the end of Psalm 135, and about two thousand years ago the rabbis who wrote the siddur copied them and placed them at the beginning of every morning and evening service.

Vintage bronze siddur.

Below is an excerpt from Psalm 135. Underline the words that are found in the בָּרְכוּ.
(Reminder: יְיָ is another way of writing God's name, יְהֹוָה.)

בֵּית יִשְׂרָאֵל בָּרְכוּ אֶת־יְהֹוָה

...בָּרוּךְ יְהֹוָה מִצִּיּוֹן.

Why do you think the rabbis chose these words from Psalms to call Jews to prayer?

_____

Imagine that you are one of the rabbis deciding how to get people to pray together. What words would you use to call people to prayer?

_____

PRAYER IN MOTION

We stand during the בָּרְכוּ and bow at the beginning of each line in the בָּרְכוּ. Bowing in prayer is a sign of respect to God.

As the leader invites the congregation to join in prayer, the leader bows from the waist while saying the word בָּרְכוּ and then stands straight when saying God's name, יְיָ. Similarly, when the congregation—and then the leader—respond, they bow from the waist on the word בָּרוּךְ and immediately stand straight as they say God's name. According to tradition, Jews stand straight when saying God's name, Adonai.

Stand up and practice bowing, and then standing straight, as you recite the בָּרְכוּ.

How can these motions help us to think more about this prayer and its meaning?

_____

_____

מַעֲרִיב עֲרָבִים

When does your day begin? When you open your eyes? Jewish days begin at sunset, which is when the evening prayer, מַעֲרִיב עֲרָבִים, is said. It praises God for creating the twilight and the darkness.

What makes the start of a new day a good time for prayer?

PRAYER
Practice reading מַעֲרִיב עֲרָבִים aloud:

1	בָּרוּךְ אַתָּה, יְיָ אֱלֹהֵינוּ,
Praised are You, Adonai our God,

2	מֶלֶךְ הָעוֹלָם, אֲשֶׁר בִּדְבָרוֹ
Ruler of the world, whose word

3 מַעֲרִיב עֲרָבִים
brings on the evening

4 בְּחָכְמָה פּוֹתֵחַ שְׁעָרִים,
and who, with wisdom, opens the gates (of heaven),

5 וּבִתְבוּנָה מְשַׁנֶּה עִתִּים,
and changes times with understanding,

6 וּמַחֲלִיף אֶת הַזְּמַנִּים,
and varies the seasons,

7 וּמְסַדֵּר אֶת הַכּוֹכָבִים,
and who arranges the stars,

8 בְּמִשְׁמְרוֹתֵיהֶם
in their stations

9 בָּרָקִיעַ כִּרְצוֹנוֹ.
in the firmament (sky) according to God's will.

10 בּוֹרֵא יוֹם וָלָיְלָה, גּוֹלֵל אוֹר
Creator of day and night, who rolls light

11 מִפְּנֵי חֹשֶׁךְ, וְחֹשֶׁךְ מִפְּנֵי אוֹר,
away from darkness, and darkness away from light,

12 וּמַעֲבִיר יוֹם וּמֵבִיא לָיְלָה,
and who causes the day to pass and brings on night,

13 וּמַבְדִּיל בֵּין יוֹם וּבֵין לָיְלָה,
and who divides between day and night,

14 יְיָ צְבָאוֹת שְׁמוֹ.
Adonai of Hosts is God's name.

15 אֵל חַי וְקַיָּם,
May the living and eternal God

rule over us always.	תָּמִיד יִמְלֹךְ עָלֵינוּ לְעוֹלָם וָעֶד.	15
Praised are You, Adonai,	בָּרוּךְ אַתָּה, יְיָ,	16
who brings on the evening.	הַמַּעֲרִיב עֲרָבִים.	17

ROOTS

The words מַעֲרִיב and עֲרָבִים look and sound similar.

These two words share the three root letters ערב. Most words with the root ערב have "being mixed with" as part of its meaning.

What do you think the connection between "evening" and "being mixed with" is?

WHAT'S IN A NAME?

Many prayers, such as the בָּרְכוּ and the שְׁמַע, get their name from the first unique one or two words of the prayer.

Read aloud the following blessings. (Circle) the name of each blessing.

בָּרוּךְ אַתָּה, יְיָ אֱלֹהֵינוּ, מֶלֶךְ הָעוֹלָם,	1
אֲשֶׁר בִּדְבָרוֹ מַעֲרִיב עֲרָבִים.	2
בָּרוּךְ אַתָּה, יְיָ אֱלֹהֵינוּ, מֶלֶךְ הָעוֹלָם,	3
שֶׁהֶחֱיָנוּ וְקִיְּמָנוּ וְהִגִּיעָנוּ לַזְּמַן הַזֶּה.	4
בָּרוּךְ אַתָּה, יְיָ אֱלֹהֵינוּ, מֶלֶךְ הָעוֹלָם,	5
הַמּוֹצִיא לֶחֶם מִן הָאָרֶץ.	6

PRAYER DICTIONARY

מַעֲרִיב
עֲרָבִים
brings on the evening

חַי
living, lives

וְקַיָּם
and eternal

יִמְלֹךְ
will rule

יוֹצֵר אוֹר

H ow would you describe a a sunrise? How would you describe a sunset differently? In what way are the sunset and sunrise partners?

מַעֲרִיב עֲרָבִים and יוֹצֵר אוֹר are "partner prayers." After the sunset, we praise God in מַעֲרִיב עֲרָבִים for bringing us evening. After the sunrise, we praise God in יוֹצֵר אוֹר for bringing us morning. Both remind us that God creates day and night, light and darkness.

Imagine that you lived at a time with no electricity. Can you think of why you would thank God for darkness? For light?

 PRAYER
Practice reading the opening and closing lines of יוֹצֵר אוֹר aloud.

Praised are You, Adonai our God,	1 בָּרוּךְ אַתָּה, יְיָ אֱלֹהֵינוּ,
Ruler of the world,	2 מֶלֶךְ הָעוֹלָם,
who forms light and creates darkness,	3 יוֹצֵר אוֹר, וּבוֹרֵא חֹשֶׁךְ,
who makes peace and creates all things.	4 עֹשֶׂה שָׁלוֹם וּבוֹרֵא אֶת הַכֹּל.
Cause a new light to shine on Zion,	5 אוֹר חָדָשׁ עַל צִיּוֹן תָּאִיר,
and may all of us be worthy to see its light.	6 וְנִזְכֶּה כֻלָּנוּ מְהֵרָה לְאוֹרוֹ.
Praised are You, Adonai,	7 בָּרוּךְ אַתָּה, יְיָ,
who forms the lights.	8 יוֹצֵר הַמְּאוֹרוֹת.

ROOTS

The root אוּר tells us that "light" is part of the word's meaning.

אוֹר means "light."

הַמְּאוֹרוֹת means "the lights."

Circle אוּר within the word הַמְּאוֹרוֹת.

The Book of Genesis tells us that God created the מְאוֹרוֹת—the sun, moon, and stars—on the fourth day of creation. Name a way that we use the light of each of these מְאוֹרוֹת.

the sun: _____

the moon: _____

the stars: _____

CREATION CONTINUES

Both מַעֲרִיב עֲרָבִים and יוֹצֵר אוֹר praise God as the Creator and describe some of God's creations.

This is what יוֹצֵר אוֹר and מַעֲרִיב עֲרָבִים say God does:

brings on the evening	מַעֲרִיב עֲרָבִים 1
forms light	יוֹצֵר אוֹר 2
makes peace	עֹשֶׂה שָׁלוֹם 3
creates all things	בּוֹרֵא אֶת הַכֹּל 4

Why do you think the prayers include so many words that mean "create"?

_____

_____

יוֹצֵר אוֹר praises God for making peace. Can you think of how making peace connects to making darkness and light?

PRAYER DICTIONARY

יוֹצֵר
forms

אוֹר
light

וּבוֹרֵא
and creates

חֹשֶׁךְ
darkness

עֹשֶׂה
makes

שָׁלוֹם
peace

הַכֹּל
all things, everything

FROM THE TEXT

Wouldn't it make more sense to say a day starts in the morning?
Why does Jewish tradition say that a day starts in the evening?

The story of Creation in the Torah describes that "... there was evening, there was morning, one day." *(Genesis 1:5)*

According to this account, when the world was first created, the day began with evening. That's why a Jewish day starts at sundown—to match the story of creation told in the Torah.

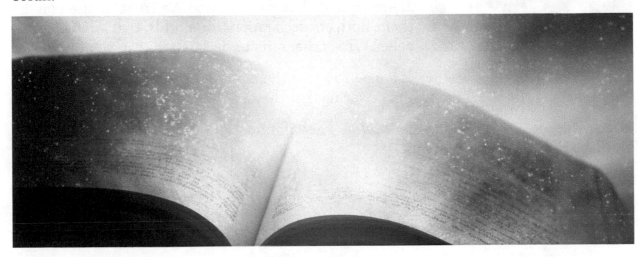

THINK ABOUT IT!

Reread the English for יוֹצֵר אוֹר and מַעֲרִיב עֲרָבִים.

Which word or phrase do you consider to be the most important in מַעֲרִיב עֲרָבִים?
Why?

_____

Which word or phrase do you consider to be the most important in יוֹצֵר אוֹר?
Why?

_____

WHERE WE ARE

Look ahead to the map of the service on page 94 and find יוֹצֵר אוֹר.

On Shabbat morning, the יוֹצֵר אוֹר blessing comes right after the _____

and before the _____ .

מַעֲרִיב עֲרָבִים / יוֹצֵר אוֹר

שְׁמַע

I n Star Wars, the Jedis say "May the force be with you." American dollars have "In God We Trust" written on them. Both are declarations, or mottos, that announce a belief. What other famous declarations can you think of?

The שְׁמַע is also a declaration. It announces that there is only one God, and to many people saying the שְׁמַע is a way of declaring that they are Jewish.

The Pledge of Allegiance, like the שְׁמַע, is a declaration. How are these two declarations similar? How are they different?

_____

_____

We say the שְׁמַע in the evening and morning services, and when we take the Torah out of the Ark. Some also say it before going to sleep, and the words of the שְׁמַע are also written on the parchment that goes inside a mezuzah.

Why do you think the שְׁמַע is recited on so many occasions and written in so many places?

_____

_____

PRAYER
Practice reading the שְׁמַע aloud:

Hear (Listen) O Israel: .... שְׁמַע יִשְׂרָאֵל: 1

Adonai is our God, Adonai is One. .... יְיָ אֱלֹהֵינוּ, יְיָ אֶחָד. 2

שְׁמַע
hear

יִשְׂרָאֵל
Israel

יְיָ
Adonai

אֱלֹהֵינוּ
our God

אֶחָד
one

א ב ג PRAYER BUILDING BLOCKS

The word שְׁמַע commands us to hear, and to listen.
If you are "listening," you're not just hearing the words, you are also understanding them.

אֱלֹהֵינוּ "our God"

אֱלֹהֵינוּ is made up of two parts:
אֱלֹהֵי means "God of."
נוּ means "us" or "our."

Look back at the קָדוֹשׁ on page 12 and (circle) all the words that have the ending נוּ. How many words did you circle?

Why do you think there are so many words in our prayers that end with נוּ?

_____

_____

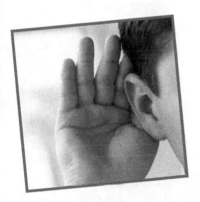

WHAT'S MISSING?

Fill in the missing English word on each line.
Practice reading the Hebrew aloud.

_____ O Israel	1 שְׁמַע
Adonai is _____	2 אֶחָד
Hear O _____	3 יִשְׂרָאֵל
_____ is our God	4 יְיָ

PRAYER IN MOTION

Many people cover their eyes when they recite the words of the שְׁמַע to help them focus on the words of this prayer.

How do you get yourself to focus and concentrate on something that is important in your life?

שְׁמַע / וְאָהַבְתָּ

PRAYER

Practice reading aloud the response to the שְׁמַע.

Blessed is the name	‫בָּרוּךְ שֵׁם‬ 1
of God's glorious kingdom	‫כְּבוֹד מַלְכוּתוֹ‬ 2
forever and ever.	‫לְעוֹלָם וָעֶד.‬ 3

Unlike the שְׁמַע these words are not from the Torah. They were first recited in the Holy Temple in Jerusalem, in response to the first line of the שְׁמַע.

If you were living in the days of the Temple, you would not have a siddur to follow along with the prayer service. Why do you think responses like this one became a set part of the prayer service?

‫בָּרוּךְ‬
blessed, praised

‫שֵׁם‬
name

‫כְּבוֹד‬
glory of

‫מַלְכוּתוֹ‬
God's kingdom

‫לְעוֹלָם וָעֶד‬
forever and ever

_____

_____

ROOTS

‫מַלְכוּתוֹ‬ is built on the root ‫מלכ‬.

The root ‫מלכ‬ means "rule." These root letters tell us that "king" or "ruler" is part of a word's meaning.

Circle the three root letters in each word.

‫מַלְכֵנוּ   מַלְכוּתוֹ   מַלְכָּה   יִמְלֹךְ   מַלְכוּת‬

Write the English meaning of ‫מַלְכוּתוֹ‬. _____

Circle the part of the English meaning that is related to the root ‫מלכ‬.

Some congregations say this response aloud while others whisper it.

How is it said in your congregation? _____

Torah crown, Russia, 1834

What do you do out of our love for someone? You might, for example, call your grandparent each week or sit with your younger brother on the school bus.

וְאָהַבְתָּ

The Torah teaches us to love God. The וְאָהַבְתָּ, which follows immediately after the שְׁמַע in the Torah and siddur, reminds us to love God by respecting and following God's commandments.

The first line of the וְאָהַבְתָּ tells us to love God with all our heart, all our soul, and all our might.

Is this an easy thing to do? What is challenging about that statement of the וְאָהַבְתָּ?

PRAYER

Practice reading the וְאָהַבְתָּ aloud:

You shall love Adonai, your God,	וְאָהַבְתָּ אֵת יְיָ אֱלֹהֶיךָ,	1
with all your heart, and with all your soul,	בְּכָל־לְבָבְךָ, וּבְכָל־נַפְשְׁךָ,	2
and with all your might.	וּבְכָל־מְאֹדֶךָ.	3
Set these words,	וְהָיוּ הַדְּבָרִים הָאֵלֶּה,	4
which I command you this day	אֲשֶׁר אָנֹכִי מְצַוְּךָ הַיּוֹם,	5
upon your heart.	עַל־לְבָבֶךָ.	6
Teach them to your children,	וְשִׁנַּנְתָּם לְבָנֶיךָ,	7
and speak of them when you are at home	וְדִבַּרְתָּ בָּם בְּשִׁבְתְּךָ בְּבֵיתֶךָ	8
and when you go on your way,	וּבְלֶכְתְּךָ בַדֶּרֶךְ,	9
and when you lie down, and when you get up.	וּבְשָׁכְבְּךָ, וּבְקוּמֶךָ.	10
Bind them as a sign upon your hand	וּקְשַׁרְתָּם לְאוֹת עַל־יָדֶךָ	11
and let them be symbols between your eyes.	וְהָיוּ לְטֹטָפֹת בֵּין עֵינֶיךָ.	12
Write them on the doorposts	וּכְתַבְתָּם עַל־מְזֻזוֹת	13
of your house and upon your gates.	בֵּיתֶךָ וּבִשְׁעָרֶיךָ.	14

שְׁמַע / וְאָהַבְתָּ

PRAYER BUILDING BLOCKS

א **ב ג** בֵּיתֶךָ "your house."

The word בֵּיתֶךָ is made up of two parts:

בַּיִת, meaning "house," and ךָ, an ending that means "you" or "your." (singular).

How many words can you find in the וְאָהַבְתָּ that end with ךָ?

Why do you think so many words in the וְאָהַבְתָּ have this ending?

ROOTS

The theme of the וְאָהַבְתָּ is our love for God. The three root letters of the word וְאָהַבְתָּ are אהב. The root אהב means "love."

Read the names of three prayers having to do with the love between God and the Jewish people:

וְאָהַבְתָּ   אַהֲבָה רַבָּה   אַהֲבַת עוֹלָם

Circle the three root letters in each of the names that tell you that "love" is part of its meaning.

Two of these prayers tell how God loves the people of Israel. The וְאָהַבְתָּ tells us to reciprocate God's love for us. Write one way that we can show our love for God.

_____

_____

וְאָהַבְתָּ
you shall love

לְבָבְךָ
your heart

הַדְּבָרִים
the words

לְאוֹת
as a sign

מְזֻזוֹת
mezuzot, doorposts

בֵּיתֶךָ
your house

Decorative mezuzah

FROM THE TEXT

The verses of the שְׁמַע and the וְאָהַבְתָּ are from chapter 6 of the Book of Deuteronomy. In this selection Moses talks to the Children of Israel about how they should behave when they enter the land of Israel.

This is how the שְׁמַע and the וְאָהַבְתָּ appear in a Torah scroll.

שְׁמַע יִשְׂרָאֵל יְהוָֹה אֱלֹהֵינוּ יְהוָֹה אֶחָד וְאָהַבְתָּ אֵת יְהוָֹה
אֱלֹהֶיךָ בְּכָל־לְבָבְךָ וּבְכָל־נַפְשְׁךָ וּבְכָל־מְאֹדֶךָ וְהָיוּ הַדְּבָרִים
הָאֵלֶּה אֲשֶׁר אָנֹכִי מְצַוְּךָ הַיּוֹם עַל־לְבָבֶךָ וְשִׁנַּנְתָּם לְבָנֶיךָ
וְדִבַּרְתָּ בָּם בְּשִׁבְתְּךָ בְּבֵיתֶךָ וּבְלֶכְתְּךָ בַדֶּרֶךְ וּבְשָׁכְבְּךָ וּבְקוּמֶךָ
וּקְשַׁרְתָּם לְאוֹת עַל־יָדֶךָ וְהָיוּ לְטֹטָפֹת בֵּין עֵינֶיךָ וּכְתַבְתָּם
עַל־מְזֻזוֹת בֵּיתֶךָ וּבִשְׁעָרֶיךָ

Find and underline the word שְׁמַע.

Draw an arrow pointing to the beginning of the וְאָהַבְתָּ, and another arrow to mark where it ends.

Was it hard or easy for you to find these words?_____

Why? _____

In the text above, (circle) the two letters in the שְׁמַע that are larger than all of the other letters.

Did you circle the last letter of the word שְׁמַע, and the last letter of the word אֶחָד?

These two letters are always written larger in Torah scrolls. Together, they form the word עֵד, meaning "witness." One of the lessons of the שְׁמַע is that each Jew has the potential to be a witness to the oneness and uniqueness of God.

How is saying that you are a witness to something different than simply telling a story to a friend?

PRAYER IN MOTION

Look at the words of the וְאָהַבְתָּ to see how they come to life in our everyday traditions. Draw a line from the sentence of the וְאָהַבְתָּ to its matching action.

Write them on the doorposts of your house and upon your gates.

וּכְתַבְתָּם עַל מְזֻזוֹת בֵּיתֶךָ וּבִשְׁעָרֶיךָ.

Some Jewish adults wear tefillin (small boxes that contain the words of the שְׁמַע and the וְאָהַבְתָּ) on their heads and arms when reciting prayers.

...and when you lie down, and when you get up.

וּבְשָׁכְבְּךָ, וּבְקוּמֶךָ...

We put the words of the שְׁמַע and the וְאָהַבְתָּ into a mezuzah case and affix it to our doorways.

Bind them as a sign upon your hand and let them be symbols between your eyes.

וּקְשַׁרְתָּם לְאוֹת עַל יָדֶךָ, וְהָיוּ לְטֹטָפֹת בֵּין עֵינֶיךָ.

It is traditional to recite the שְׁמַע and the וְאָהַבְתָּ every morning and evening.

The וְאָהַבְתָּ also instructs us to "teach them to your children." What is an important value or tradition that your parent or grandparent has taught you?

_____

_____

Which Jewish traditions and values do you hope to teach your children?

_____

WHERE WE ARE

Look ahead to page 94 and find the שְׁמַע and the וְאָהַבְתָּ.

On Shabbat morning, the שְׁמַע and the וְאָהַבְתָּ come right after the _____

and before the _____ .

Wow! Have you ever said, "Wow" and really meant it? What made you say it? Was it something that seemed impossible but somehow happened anyway? Some people call these kinds of experiences "miracles."

The story of how the Sea of Reeds split in half and allowed the Israelites to escape is a miracle described in the Torah. Afterwards, the Israelites sang מִי כָמֹכָה—meaning "Who is like You?"—praising God's awesome power. The words of the מִי כָמֹכָה prayer come from that song.

The last time you had a "Wow" moment, what did you say afterwards?

PRAYER

Practice reading the מִי כָמֹכָה aloud:

1	מִי־כָמֹכָה בָּאֵלִם יְיָ?
2	מִי כָמֹכָה נֶאְדָּר בַּקֹּדֶשׁ?
3	נוֹרָא תְהִלֹּת, עֹשֵׂה פֶלֶא?
4	שִׁירָה חֲדָשָׁה שִׁבְּחוּ גְאוּלִים
5	לְשִׁמְךָ עַל שְׂפַת הַיָּם
6	יַחַד כֻּלָּם הוֹדוּ
7	וְהִמְלִיכוּ וְאָמְרוּ:
8	יְיָ יִמְלֹךְ לְעוֹלָם וָעֶד.
9	צוּר יִשְׂרָאֵל
10	קוּמָה בְּעֶזְרַת יִשְׂרָאֵל
11	וּפְדֵה כִנְאֻמֶךָ יְהוּדָה וְיִשְׂרָאֵל.
12	גֹּאֲלֵנוּ יְיָ צְבָאוֹת שְׁמוֹ,
13	קְדוֹשׁ יִשְׂרָאֵל.
14	בָּרוּךְ אַתָּה יְיָ, גָּאַל יִשְׂרָאֵל.

Who is like You among the gods, Adonai? .... (1)

Who is like You, majestic in holiness? .... (2)

Awesome in splendor, doing wonders? .... (3)

(With) a new song the redeemed people .... (4)

praised Your name by the shore of the sea. .... (5)

Together all of them gave thanks to You .... (6)

and they declared You their Sovereign and they said: (7)

May Adonai reign forever and ever. (8)

Rock of Israel, (9)

arise and bring help to Israel, ... (10)

and, as You pronounced, redeem Judah and Israel. ...... (11)

Our Redeemer, Adonai of hosts is God's name, ... (12)

the Holy One of Israel. .... (13)

Blessed are You, Adonai, who redeemed Israel. ...... (14)

THREE KINDS OF PRAYER

Most of our prayers praise God, make a request of God, or thank God. Some prayers even do all three.

Do you think the מִי כָמֹכָה is a prayer of praise, a prayer of asking for something, or a prayer of thanks? Remember, it may be more than one kind of prayer.

_____

Show evidence from the prayer to support your answer.

_____

_____

What kinds of nearly impossible events or actions have you observed or heard about? What made them seem impossible? Do you think they were miracles? Why?

_____

_____

WHERE WE ARE

Look ahead to page 94 and find the מִי כָמֹכָה. On Shabbat morning, the מִי כָמֹכָה comes right after the

_____

and before the _____.

Look ahead to page 94 and find the מִי כָמֹכָה.

PRAYER DICTIONARY

מִי
who

כָמֹכָה,
כָּמֹכָה
like you

בָּאֵלִם
*among the gods
(other nations
worship)*

יְיָ
Adonai

נֶאְדָּר
majestic

בַּקֹּדֶשׁ
in (the) holiness

THANK YOU!

🌱 ROOTS

The word בַּקֹדֶשׁ is built on the root קדשׁ. The root קדשׁ means "holy."

The root קדשׁ tells us that "holy" is part of the word's meaning.

(Circle) the three root letters in בַּקֹדֶשׁ.

Write the root. ___ ___ ___

What does the root mean?_____

Read the following words aloud. (Circle) the three root letters in each of these words.

קָדוֹשׁ   קָדְשׁוֹ   וְתִתְקַדַּשׁ   הַקָּדוֹשׁ   קִדְּשָׁנוּ

(*Reminder: the* ָ *in* קָדְשׁוֹ *is pronounced "oh."*)

In many blessings we praise God for making us holy—קִדְּשָׁנוּ—through God's commandments. People are holy, places are holy, time is holy, and some things are holy. What do you consider holy?

_____ is a holy place.

_____ is a holy time.

_____ is a holy object.

יִמְלֹךְ—meaning "will rule"—is built on the root מלכ.

The root מלכ means "rule." These root letters tell us that "king" or "ruler" is part of a word's meaning.

(Circle) the three root letters in יִמְלֹךְ.

Which line on page 33 has the word יִמְלֹךְ?_____

מִי כָמֹכָה

BUILDING YOUR VOCABULARY

Circle the Hebrew word or phrase that means the same as the English.

like you	סִדּוּר	כָּמֹכָה	שָׁמַע
Adonai	מִי	בָּאֵלִם	יְיָ
majestic	בַּקֹּדֶשׁ	יִשְׂרָאֵל	נֶאְדָּר
who	מִי	אֶחָד	שֵׁם
in (the) holiness	בָּרְכוּ	בַּקֹּדֶשׁ	בָּאֵלִם
among the gods [other nations worship]	בָּאֵלִם	הַמְבֹרָךְ	לְעוֹלָם וָעֶד

THE HOLIDAY CONNECTION

Legend has it that in order to inspire the Jews to join together and fight King Antiochus, Judah, the Jewish leader, called out the first words of the מִי כָמֹכָה. The first letters of these words then became the freedom fighters' nick-name—the Maccabees. We celebrate the victory of the Maccabees on Hanukkah. And some people believe that the story of Hanukkah—where one little pitcher of olive oil provided enough oil for the menorah to be lit for eight long days—is another miracle!

Write the first letter of each Hebrew word in the spaces below.

מִי כָמֹכָה בָּאֵלִם יְיָ ____ ____ ____

What does this word spell?

Why do you think Judah chose these words to rally the Jews together?

_____

_____

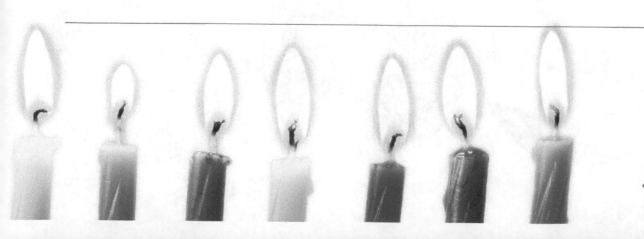

Below is a page from the Book of Exodus. It shows the Song of the Sea, the song the Israelites sang after they crossed the Sea of Reeds.

According to the Torah, the waters of the Sea of Reeds formed a wall to the right and to the left of the Israelites as they crossed on dry land. Some people think that the Song of the Sea is written like an open wall of brickwork, reminding them of the walls of water on either side of the Israelites. Some say it looks like waves hitting an unseen barrier.

What do you think the text looks like?

Find and read the first three lines of the מִי כָמֹכָה. (Circle) these lines.

Find and read another phrase that appears in the מִי כָמֹכָה.
(Hint: The word יִמְלֹךְ is in the phrase.) Underline this phrase.

9 אָמַר		
אוֹיֵב אֶרְדֹּף אַשִּׂיג	אֲחַלֵּק שָׁלָל תִּמְלָאֵמוֹ	
נַפְשִׁי	אָרִיק חַרְבִּי תּוֹרִישֵׁמוֹ יָדִי:	נָשַׁפְתָּ
בְרוּחֲךָ כִּסָּמוֹ יָם	צָלֲלוּ כַּעוֹפֶרֶת בְּמַיִם	
אַדִּירִים: 11 מִי	מִי־כָמֹכָה בָּאֵלִם יְהֹוָה	
כָּמֹכָה נֶאְדָּר בַּקֹּדֶשׁ	נוֹרָא תְהִלֹּת עֹשֵׂה־	
פֶלֶא: 12 13 נָחִיתָ	נָטִיתָ יְמִינְךָ תִּבְלָעֵמוֹ אָרֶץ:	
בְחַסְדְּךָ עַם־זוּ גָּאָלְתָּ	נֵהַלְתָּ בְעָזְּךָ אֶל־נְוֵה	
קָדְשֶׁךָ: 14 חִיל	שָׁמְעוּ עַמִּים יִרְגָּזוּן	
אָחַז יֹשְׁבֵי פְּלָשֶׁת: 15	אָז נִבְהֲלוּ אַלּוּפֵי	
אֱדוֹם	אֵילֵי מוֹאָב יֹאחֲזֵמוֹ רָעַד	נָמֹגוּ
16 כֹּל יֹשְׁבֵי כְנָעַן:	תִּפֹּל עֲלֵיהֶם אֵימָתָה	
וָפַחַד	בִּגְדֹל זְרוֹעֲךָ יִדְּמוּ כָּאָבֶן	עַד־
יַעֲבֹר עַמְּךָ יְהֹוָה	עַד־יַעֲבֹר עַם־זוּ	
קָנִיתָ: 17 מָכוֹן	תְּבִאֵמוֹ וְתִטָּעֵמוֹ בְּהַר נַחֲלָתְךָ	
לְשִׁבְתְּךָ פָּעַלְתָּ יְהֹוָה	מִקְּדָשׁ אֲדֹנָי כּוֹנְנוּ	
18 19 יָדֶיךָ:	יְהֹוָה ׀ יִמְלֹךְ לְעֹלָם וָעֶד:	

PRAYER IN MOTION

The מִי כָמֹכָה is part of the final blessing recited after the שְׁמַע and just before the עֲמִידָה.

It is traditional to rise toward the end of the blessing, as we sing these words:

צוּר יִשְׂרָאֵל, קוּמָה בְּעֶזְרַת יִשְׂרָאֵל

Rock of Israel, arise and bring help to Israel

We then remain standing for the next prayer, the עֲמִידָה.

On page 33, put an ↑ next to the words on which we rise.

How might knowing traditions, such as when your congregation stands or sits, help you feel more comfortable in a service and build your connection with others in the community?

_____

_____

AN ETHICAL ECHO

The Israelites sang מִי כָמֹכָה to praise God for bringing them out of Egypt. Throughout our history, the Jewish people have experienced captivity and freedom, slavery and independence. We know how precious freedom is. And many of us are determined to rescue those who are not free.

We call this the mitzvah of *Pidyon Shevuyim*—פִּדְיוֹן שְׁבוּיִים—Redeeming Captives.

Name one way in which you can help bring freedom to other people in the world.

_____

Research online to learn about Jewish organizations that are working today to free people from slavery or other dangerous conditions.

An organization I learned about is: _____

This organization helps people by:

_____

_____

אָבוֹת

Who are you? When someone asks you that, how do you answer? Maybe you also mention a relationship, like "I'm Nathan's brother." Similarly, the אָבוֹת asks God to recognize us in relation to our ancestors Abraham, Isaac, and Jacob.

The אָבוֹת is the first blessing of the Amidah, a group of blessings at the heart of every prayer service. It praises God for watching over us just as God watched over our ancestors.

Why do you think the Amidah begins with our identifying ourselves as the descendants of Abraham, Isaac, and Jacob?

PRAYER
Practice reading the אָבוֹת aloud:

Praised are You, Adonai,	בָּרוּךְ אַתָּה יְיָ,	1
our God and God of our fathers,	אֱלֹהֵינוּ וֵאלֹהֵי אֲבוֹתֵינוּ,	2
God of Abraham, God of Isaac,	אֱלֹהֵי אַבְרָהָם, אֱלֹהֵי יִצְחָק,	3
and God of Jacob.	וֵאלֹהֵי יַעֲקֹב.	4
The great, mighty and awesome God,	הָאֵל הַגָּדוֹל, הַגִּבּוֹר, וְהַנּוֹרָא,	5
supreme God. You do acts of loving-kindness	אֵל עֶלְיוֹן. גּוֹמֵל חֲסָדִים טוֹבִים	6
and create everything and remember	וְקוֹנֵה הַכֹּל, וְזוֹכֵר	7
the kindnesses of the fathers,	חַסְדֵי אָבוֹת,	8
and You will bring a redeemer	וּמֵבִיא גוֹאֵל	9
to their children's children,	לִבְנֵי בְנֵיהֶם,	10
for the sake of Your name, and in love.	לְמַעַן שְׁמוֹ בְּאַהֲבָה.	11
Ruler, Helper, Rescuer, and Shield.	מֶלֶךְ עוֹזֵר וּמוֹשִׁיעַ וּמָגֵן.	12
Praised are You, Adonai, Shield of Abraham.	בָּרוּךְ אַתָּה יְיָ, מָגֵן אַבְרָהָם.	13

אָבוֹת וְאִמָּהוֹת

Who is in your family tree? The Jewish people's family tree begins with Abraham, Sarah, Isaac, Rebecca, Jacob, Rachel and Leah.

The original אָבוֹת prayer just included the patriarchs. Today, many congregations now include the אִמָּהוֹת—the matriarchs—as well. Whether the Amidah includes just the אָבוֹת or also the אִמָּהוֹת, it reminds us that, according to tradition, we merit God's favor because of our link to our ancestors' goodness, and faith.

Does your congregation include the אִמָּהוֹת when reciting the Amidah?

 PRAYER

Practice reading the אָבוֹת וְאִמָּהוֹת aloud:

Praised are You, Adonai, our God	בָּרוּךְ אַתָּה יְיָ, אֱלֹהֵינוּ 1
and God of our fathers and mothers,	וֵאלֹהֵי אֲבוֹתֵינוּ וְאִמּוֹתֵינוּ, 2
God of Abraham, God of Isaac,	אֱלֹהֵי אַבְרָהָם, אֱלֹהֵי יִצְחָק, 3
and God of Jacob, God of Sarah,	וֵאלֹהֵי יַעֲקֹב, אֱלֹהֵי שָׂרָה, 4
God of Rebecca, God of Leah	אֱלֹהֵי רִבְקָה, אֱלֹהֵי לֵאָה 5
and God of Rachel.	וֵאלֹהֵי רָחֵל. 6
The great, mighty and awesome God,	הָאֵל הַגָּדוֹל, הַגִּבּוֹר, וְהַנּוֹרָא, 7
supreme God. You do acts of loving-kindness	אֵל עֶלְיוֹן. גּוֹמֵל חֲסָדִים טוֹבִים 8
and create everything and remember	וְקוֹנֵה הַכֹּל, וְזוֹכֵר 9
the kindnesses of the fathers and mothers	חַסְדֵי אָבוֹת וְאִמָּהוֹת, 10
and You will bring a redeemer / redemption	וּמֵבִיא גּוֹאֵל / גְּאֻלָּה 11

אָבוֹת
fathers

אֲבוֹתֵינוּ
our fathers

אֱלֹהֵי
God of

אַבְרָהָם
Abraham

יִצְחָק
Isaac

יַעֲקֹב
Jacob

12 לִבְנֵי בְנֵיהֶם, ... *to their children's children*

13 לְמַעַן שְׁמוֹ בְּאַהֲבָה. *for the sake of Your name, and in love.*

14 מֶלֶךְ עוֹזֵר .... *Ruler, Helper*

15 וּמוֹשִׁיעַ וּמָגֵן. .... *Rescuer, and Shield.*

16 בָּרוּךְ אַתָּה יְיָ, ... *Praised are You, Adonai,*

17 מָגֵן אַבְרָהָם .... *Shield of Abraham*

18 וּפֹקֵד/וְעֶזְרַת שָׂרָה. .... *and Protector/Help of Sarah.*

BUILDING YOUR VOCABULARY

Read the Hebrew words aloud. Circle the Hebrew word that means the same as the English.

fathers	אַבְרָהָם	אָבוֹת	אוֹר
our fathers	אֲבוֹתֵינוּ	אֱלֹהֵינוּ	אַתָּה
God of	יִשְׂרָאֵל	וְאָהַבְתָּ	אֱלֹהֵי

NAME GAME

Write the English name of each of the fathers.

אַבְרָהָם _____

יִצְחָק _____

יַעֲקֹב _____

PRAYER VARIATIONS

Some congregations pray for God to bring a redeemer (גּוֹאֵל)—the Messiah—who will bring peace to the world, while other congregations pray for redemption (גְּאֻלָה)—a state of peace and perfection in the world. But all Jews are alike in praying for a better and more peaceful world.

Some congregations express God's loyalty to Sarah by describing God as her Protector (וּפֹקֵד שָׂרָה). Others speak of God as Sarah's Help (וְעֶזְרַת שָׂרָה).

BUILDING YOUR VOCABULARY

Read the Hebrew words aloud. Circle the Hebrew word that means the same as the English.

mothers	הָאֲדָמָה	אִמָהוֹת	אֱמֶת
our mothers	הָאָרֶץ	אֵלִיָהוּ	אִמוֹתֵינוּ
God of	אֱלֹהֵי	אַבְרָהָם	אָרוֹן

NAME GAME

Write the English name of each of the mothers.

שָׂרָה _____

רִבְקָה _____

לֵאָה _____

רָחֵל _____

PRAYER DICTIONARY

אִמָהוֹת
mothers

אִמוֹתֵינוּ
our mothers

אֱלֹהֵי
God of

שָׂרָה
Sarah

רִבְקָה
Rebecca

לֵאָה
Leah

רָחֵל
Rachel

The Cave of Machpelah, Sarah's Tomb, Hebron

In the אָבוֹת וְאִמָּהוֹת, God is not simply referred to as God.
Rather, the prayer is directed to "our God, God of our fathers and mothers, God of Abraham, God of Isaac, God of Jacob, God of Sarah, God of Rebecca, God of Leah, and God of Rachel."

It seems repetitive, doesn't it? Why do you think it mentions the relationship of God to each of our ancestors?

_____

_____

_____

_____

WHAT'S IN A NAME?

The עֲמִידָה, which begins with the אָבוֹת blessing, is the heart and center of every synagogue service. The עֲמִידָה has many names:

- **Amidah** — עֲמִידָה means "standing."
  We always stand when we say the עֲמִידָה.
  It is as if we are standing before God.

- **The Silent Prayer** — It is called this because many people say it
  in a very quiet voice. They are talking privately to God.

- **The שְׁמוֹנֶה עֶשְׂרֵה** (the Hebrew for "eighteen") —
  Originally, the weekday עֲמִידָה contained eighteen blessings.
  Now it consists of nineteen blessings (when it is said on a weekday)
  or seven blessings (when it is said on Shabbat and holidays).

The עֲמִידָה is so important that many congregations simply call it the "Prayer" (תְּפִלָּה).

What name do you think is most appropriate for the עֲמִידָה? Why?

_____

_____

אָבוֹת / אָבוֹת וְאִמָּהוֹת

GOD'S GREATNESS

The אָבוֹת uses four words to describe God's greatness.
Write the English meaning for each one.

עֶלְיוֹן	וְהַנּוֹרָא	הַגִּבּוֹר	הַגָּדוֹל

The אָבוֹת identifies four roles that God plays in the lives of the Jewish people.

Write the English meaning for each one.

וּמָגֵן	וּמוֹשִׁיעַ	עוֹזֵר	מֶלֶךְ

FROM THE TEXT

Read this selection from the Torah (*Deuteronomy 10:17*).
Underline the words similar to those in the אָבוֹת that describe God's greatness.

וַאֲדֹנֵי הָאֲדֹנִים הָאֵל הַגָּדֹל הַגִּבֹּר וְהַנּוֹרָא

Why do you think the Torah and the אָבוֹת use so many different words to describe God's greatness?

_____

_____

In the phrase חֲסָדִים טוֹבִים the word טוֹבִים helps us know how good the acts of loving-kindness are. What are some acts of loving-kindness that we can do to partner with God?

_____

_____

הַגָּדוֹל
the great

הַגִּבּוֹר
the mighty

וְהַנּוֹרָא
and the awesome

עֶלְיוֹן
supreme

חֲסָדִים טוֹבִים
acts of loving-kindness

מֶלֶךְ
ruler

עוֹזֵר
helper

וּמוֹשִׁיעַ
and rescuer

וּמָגֵן
and shield

FAMILY TREE

Abraham, Isaac, and Jacob are called the אָבוֹת ("fathers") of Judaism.
Sarah, Rebecca, Leah, and Rachel are called the אִמָּהוֹת ("mothers") of Judaism.
They were the first family to believe in one God.

Fill in the missing English words and names on our ancestors' family tree.

אָבוֹת	&	אִמָּהוֹת

| _____ | | _____ |
| אַבְרָהָם | | שָׂרָה |

| Isaac | | Rebecca |
| יִצְחָק | | רִבְקָה |

| _____ | | _____ |
| יַעֲקֹב | | רָחֵל   לֵאָה |

PRAYER IN MOTION

When we say the עֲמִידָה we are addressing God with our prayer.
It is as if we are in the presence of a king or a queen, so we behave in a respectful way.

In some synagogues we:

1. Stand.

2. Face toward Jerusalem, where the Temple once stood.

3. Take three small steps backwards, and three more steps forward before we begin.

4. Bow at the beginning and end of the אָבוֹת.

5. Bow several more times at specific parts of the עֲמִידָה.

6. Don't stop to talk while reading the prayer.

7. Take three small steps backwards and three more forward when we finish the prayer.

How do you think these actions can help us concentrate when reciting the Amidah?

גְּבוּרוֹת

In the comics, Superman can fly and Wonder Woman has super-strength. According to גְּבוּרוֹת ("powers"), the second blessing of the עֲמִידָה, God has even more awesome powers than that: God gives us each life, helps the falling, heals the sick, and frees captives.

Which of God's powers do you think is the most important? Why?

 PRAYER
Practice reading the גְּבוּרוֹת aloud:

1	אַתָּה גִּבּוֹר לְעוֹלָם, אֲדֹנָי,
You are eternally mighty (powerful), Adonai,	
2	מְחַיֵּה הַכֹּל/מֵתִים אַתָּה,
You give life to all/the dead,	
3	רַב לְהוֹשִׁיעַ.
great is Your power to save.	
4	מְכַלְכֵּל חַיִּים בְּחֶסֶד,
With kindness You sustain the living,	
5	מְחַיֵּה הַכֹּל/מֵתִים
give life to all/the dead	
6	בְּרַחֲמִים רַבִּים.
with great compassion (mercy).	
7	סוֹמֵךְ נוֹפְלִים, וְרוֹפֵא חוֹלִים,
You help the falling, and heal the sick,	
8	וּמַתִּיר אֲסוּרִים, וּמְקַיֵּם
and You free the captive, and keep	
9	אֱמוּנָתוֹ לִישֵׁנֵי עָפָר.
faith with those who sleep in the dust.	
10	מִי כָמוֹךָ, בַּעַל גְּבוּרוֹת,
Who is like You, God of Power,	
11	וּמִי דוֹמֶה לָךְ,
and who is comparable to You,	
12	מֶלֶךְ מֵמִית וּמְחַיֶּה
Ruler who brings death and gives life	
13	וּמַצְמִיחַ יְשׁוּעָה?
and who is a source of salvation?	
14	וְנֶאֱמָן אַתָּה לְהַחֲיוֹת
You are faithful to give life	
15	הַכֹּל/מֵתִים. בָּרוּךְ אַתָּה יְיָ,
to all/the dead. Praised are You, Adonai	
16	מְחַיֵּה הַכֹּל/הַמֵּתִים.
who gives life to all/the dead.	

אַתָּה
you

גִּבּוֹר
mighty, powerful

לְעוֹלָם
eternally

מְחַיֶּה
gives life

לְהוֹשִׁיעַ
to save

חַיִּים
life, the living

בְּרַחֲמִים
*with compassion,
mercy*

מִי כָמוֹךָ
who is like You?

BUILDING YOUR VOCABULARY

Read each of the Hebrew words aloud. Then (circle) the Hebrew word or phrase that means the same as the English.

who is like You?	מִי כָמוֹךָ	וְעַל	וְהַנּוֹרָא
life, the living	אֱמֶת	זִכָּרוֹן	חַיִּים
eternally	עֶלְיוֹן	לְעוֹלָם	הַגָּדוֹל
mighty, powerful	גִּבּוֹר	גּוֹמֵל	מֶלֶךְ
You	אֶחָד	אַתָּה	אָבוֹת
give life	מְחַיֶּה	מוֹשִׁיעַ	מָגֵן
with compassion, mercy	וּבְרָצוֹן	בְּרַחֲמִים	בְּאַהֲבָה
to save	לְהוֹשִׁיעַ	לִיצִיאַת	לְהַדְלִיק

PRAYER VARIATIONS

Reform and Reconstructionist prayer books use the phrases מְחַיֶּה כֹּל חַי and מְחַיֶּה הַכֹּל ("gives life to everything") in the גְבוּרוֹת. Conservative and Orthodox prayer books contain the words מְחַיֶּה הַמֵּתִים ("revives the dead").

The concept of "reviving the dead" is called resurrection. Belief in resurrection is the belief that, at some time in the future, all those who have died will be brought back to life by God. Some people interpret the phrase "reviving the dead" symbolically, and use it to refer to the cycle of nature. For example, plants that are dormant and animals that hibernate in the winter become active again in the spring. Some interpret it as an expression of our belief that the good we have done will live on in the hearts and minds of others.

Which version of the גְבוּרוֹת does your congregation's prayer book include?

WHAT'S IN A NAME?

Like the אָבוֹת, the גְּבוּרוֹת gets its name from the main theme of the blessing—God's powers.

We begin this blessing with the words אַתָּה גִבּוֹר לְעוֹלָם, "you are eternally mighty (powerful)."

Which three root letters are in the word גִבּוֹר and the name of the blessing, גְּבוּרוֹת? (Remember: בּ and ב are family letters.) ___ ___ ___

The גְּבוּרוֹת praises God's power, or ability, to:

1. *create life*   2. *save life*   3. *sustain life*

4. *help the falling*   5. *heal the sick*   6. *free the captive*

The Torah tells us that we are created in God's image—בְּצֶלֶם אֱלֹהִים (Genesis 1:27). From this verse we understand that we have the ability and the responsibility to act in godly ways.

Choose three of God's powers, as described in the גְּבוּרוֹת, from the list above, and give an example of what people can do to act in God's image. Here is one example:

1. *Heal the sick—We can become doctors or nurses who work to cure illness and disease.*

2. _____

3. _____

In the אָבוֹת, we praise God for doing acts of loving-kindness—חֲסָדִים טוֹבִים. And in the גְּבוּרוֹת, we praise God for sustaining the living with kindness—בְּחֶסֶד.

Which three root letters tell us that "kindness" is part of a word's meaning?

___ ___ ___

Is it important that an action be done with kindness? Why or why not?

_____

🌱 ROOTS

The root letters of מְחַיֶּה and חַיִּים are חיה.

The root חיה tells us that "life" is part of a word's meaning.

Sometimes, like in the word חַיִּים, the final root letter ה drops out of a word.

מְחַיֶּה means _____ .

חַיִּים means _____ .

Look back at the גְּבוּרוֹת blessing on page 46. (Circle) all the words with the root חיה.

How many words did you circle? _____

Why do you think this root appears so many times in this blessing?

_____

The root of בְּרַחֲמִים is רחמ. The root רחמ tells us that "compassion or mercy" is part of a word's meaning. בְּרַחֲמִים means "with compassion, mercy."

God is sometimes referred to as אֵל מָלֵא רַחֲמִים.

This means "God, full of _____ ."

Below are three other names by which God is known.
(Circle) the root letters רחמ in each.

אַב הָרַחֲמִים
The Merciful Parent

אֵל חַנּוּן וְרַחוּם
**Gracious and
Compassionate God**

הָרַחֲמָן
The Merciful One

What is one way you can imitate God,
act in God's image, by being compassionate?

_____

_____

גְּבוּרוֹת / קְדוּשָׁה

קְדוּשָׁה

The word קְדוּשָׁה means "holiness." But what does holiness mean? Our tradition describes Shabbat as a holy time, Jerusalem as a holy city, and Israel as a holy people. What do you think those three things have in common that makes them holy?

Circle all the phrases in the text below that say God is holy. How many are there?_____

Let us sanctify Your name in the world,	נְקַדֵּשׁ אֶת שִׁמְךָ בָּעוֹלָם, 1
as they sanctify it in the highest heavens,	כְּשֵׁם שֶׁמַּקְדִּישִׁים אוֹתוֹ בִּשְׁמֵי מָרוֹם, 2
as it is written by Your prophet, and one called	כַּכָּתוּב עַל יַד נְבִיאֶךָ: וְקָרָא 3
to another and said: "Holy, Holy, Holy	זֶה אֶל זֶה וְאָמַר: קָדוֹשׁ, קָדוֹשׁ, קָדוֹשׁ 4
is Adonai of the heavenly legions,	יְיָ צְבָאוֹת, 5
the whole earth is full of God's glory"	מְלֹא כָל הָאָרֶץ כְּבוֹדוֹ. 6
You are majestic, Adonai, our God. How	אַדִּיר אַדִּירֵנוּ, יְיָ אֲדוֹנֵנוּ, מָה 7
powerful is Your name throughout the earth.	אַדִּיר שִׁמְךָ בְּכָל הָאָרֶץ. 8
Praised is the glory of God from God's heavenly place.	בָּרוּךְ כְּבוֹד יְיָ מִמְּקוֹמוֹ. 9
Our God is one, God is our Parent,	אֶחָד הוּא אֱלֹהֵינוּ, הוּא אָבִינוּ, 10
God is our Ruler, God is our Rescuer,	הוּא מַלְכֵּנוּ, הוּא מוֹשִׁיעֵנוּ, 11
And with mercy God will declare	וְהוּא יַשְׁמִיעֵנוּ בְּרַחֲמָיו שֵׁנִית 12
before all the living,	לְעֵינֵי כָּל חָי, לִהְיוֹת לָכֶם לֵאלֹהִים, 13
I am Adonai, your God. Adonai will rule	אֲנִי יְיָ אֱלֹהֵיכֶם. יִמְלֹךְ יְיָ 14
forever; your God, O Zion, from generation	לְעוֹלָם, אֱלֹהַיִךְ צִיּוֹן, לְדֹר 15
to generation. Halleluyah! From generation	וָדֹר, הַלְלוּיָהּ. לְדוֹר 16
to generation we will tell of Your greatness,	וָדוֹר נַגִּיד גָּדְלֶךָ, 17
and for all eternity we will proclaim Your holiness.	וּלְנֵצַח נְצָחִים קְדֻשָּׁתְךָ נַקְדִּישׁ 18
And our praise of You, our God,	וְשִׁבְחֲךָ, אֱלֹהֵינוּ, 19
will not depart from our mouths forever and ever.	מִפִּינוּ לֹא יָמוּשׁ לְעוֹלָם וָעֶד, 20
Praised are You, Adonai, the holy God.	בָּרוּךְ אַתָּה יְיָ, הָאֵל הַקָּדוֹשׁ. 21

PRAYER DICTIONARY

נְקַדֵּשׁ
let us sanctify

שִׁמְךָ
your name

כְּבוֹדוֹ
God's glory

יִמְלֹךְ
will rule

לְדוֹר וָדֹר
from generation to generation

נַגִּיד
we will tell

גָּדְלְךָ
your greatness

BUILDING YOUR VOCABULARY

Below, the list on the right includes the words from the קְדוּשָׁה. The list on the left includes words you have already learned.

Draw lines to connect the related words.
(Hint: Look for common roots.)

הַגָּדוֹל	נְקַדֵּשׁ	1
הַגָּדָה	יִמְלֹךְ	2
כָּבוֹד	גָּדְלֶךָ	3
מֶלֶךְ	שִׁמְךָ	4
קָדוֹשׁ	כְּבוֹדוֹ	5
שֵׁם	נַגִּיד	6

FROM THE TEXT

At the heart of the קְדוּשָׁה are three verses that come from different places in the תַּנַ"ךְ (Bible): Isaiah, Ezekiel and Psalms.

The first of these verses was spoken by the prophet Isaiah as he described a mystical vision of God sitting on the Divine Throne surrounded by angels. As the angels moved their wings, they called to one another and said:

קָדוֹשׁ, קָדוֹשׁ, קָדוֹשׁ יְיָ צְבָאוֹת, מְלֹא כָל הָאָרֶץ כְּבוֹדוֹ.

Holy, Holy, Holy is Adonai of the heavenly legions, the whole earth is full of God's glory. (Isaiah 6:3)

What do you think it means that "the whole earth is full of God's glory"?

_____

_____

א PRAYER BUILDING BLOCKS
פ ב ג נְקַדֵּשׁ אֶת שִׁמְךָ בָּעוֹלָם "let us sanctify your name in the world"

נְקַדֵּשׁ means "let us sanctify." Another way of saying "sanctify" is "make holy." נְקַדֵּשׁ is built on the root קדשׁ.

Words built on the root קדשׁ have _____ as part of their meaning.

שִׁמְךָ means "your name."

שֵׁם means _____.

ךָ at the end of a word means _____.

Whose name are we sanctifying? _____.

בָּעוֹלָם means "in the world."

בָּ means _____.

עוֹלָם means_____.

Look back at the קְדוּשָׁה on page 50. (Circle) all the words with the root קדשׁ.

How many words did you circle?_____

Why do you think there are so many words with the root קדשׁ?

_____

PRAYER IN MOTION

When the עֲמִידָה is recited in a minyan—a group of ten Jewish adults—we say the קְדוּשָׁה out loud, while standing tall and straight with our feet together.

It is as if we are echoing the angels in the prophet Isaiah's vision. As we recite the words קָדוֹשׁ, קָדוֹשׁ, קָדוֹשׁ we rise up on our toes three times and imagine that we are elevating ourselves in the same way that the angels were elevated in God's eyes.

WHERE WE ARE

The עֲמִידָה is part of every prayer service. The first three blessings of every עֲמִידָה are blessings of praise and the last three are blessings of thanks. These opening and closing blessings are always the same. The middle blessings change. Weekdays, Shabbat and holidays have a different set of middle blessings.

Complete the chart below about the first three blessings of the עֲמִידָה.

	HEBREW NAME	THEME OR SUBJECT OF BLESSING
1st blessing		
2nd blessing		
3rd blessing		

Look ahead at page 94 and find the first three blessings of the עֲמִידָה.

On Shabbat morning, these three blessings come right after the _____

and right before _____ .

שָׁלוֹם רָב

שָׁלוֹם! When someone says שָׁלוֹם, they could be saying "Hi" or "Goodbye." It is also the word for our greatest hope: שָׁלוֹם—peace.

When the Jewish people make a wish as a community, it is often a wish for peace, שָׁלוֹם. The idea of שָׁלוֹם is so important that in the morning, afternoon, and evening we close the Amidah by asking God for peace. In the afternoon and evening service, we begin this blessing with the words שָׁלוֹם רָב ("great peace"). In the morning, the blessing begins with the words שִׂים שָׁלוֹם ("grant peace").

Why do you think Hebrew has the same word for hello, goodbye and peace?

📖 PRAYER

Practice reading שָׁלוֹם רָב aloud:

May You grant great peace	שָׁלוֹם רָב	1
upon Israel Your people	עַל־יִשְׂרָאֵל עַמְּךָ	2
(and upon all who live on the earth)	**(וְעַל כָּל־יוֹשְׁבֵי תֵבֵל)**	3
forever, for You are	תָּשִׂים לְעוֹלָם, כִּי אַתָּה הוּא	4
the Ruler, Sovereign of all peace.	מֶלֶךְ אָדוֹן לְכָל־הַשָּׁלוֹם.	5
And may it be good in Your eyes to bless	וְטוֹב בְּעֵינֶיךָ לְבָרֵךְ	6
Your people Israel (and all peoples)	אֶת־עַמְּךָ יִשְׂרָאֵל (וְאֶת־כָּל־הָעַמִּים)	7
at every time and every hour with Your peace.	בְּכָל־עֵת וּבְכָל־שָׁעָה בִּשְׁלוֹמֶךָ.	8
Praised are You, Adonai,	בָּרוּךְ אַתָּה, יְיָ,	9
who blesses God's people	הַמְבָרֵךְ אֶת־עַמּוֹ	10
Israel with peace.	יִשְׂרָאֵל בַּשָּׁלוֹם.	11

א PRAYER BUILDING BLOCKS
פ ג שָׁלוֹם רָב עַל־יִשְׂרָאֵל "great peace upon Israel"

שָׁלוֹם
peace

רָב
great

יִשְׂרָאֵל
Israel

עַמְּךָ
your people

וְטוֹב
*and may it
be good*

בְּעֵינֶיךָ
in your eyes

לְבָרֵךְ
to bless

בְּשְׁלוֹמֶךָ
with your peace

שָׁלוֹם רָב means "great peace."

In Hebrew, the word שָׁלוֹם means more than just "peace."

The root שלמ tells us that "peace," "harmony," "completedness," or "wholeness" is part of a word's meaning.

בְּשְׁלוֹמֶךָ means "with your peace."

(Circle) the root letters שלמ in the word בְּשְׁלוֹמֶךָ.

What connections do you see between peace and wholeness?

_____

_____

עַל־יִשְׂרָאֵל עַמְּךָ "upon Israel Your people"

יִשְׂרָאֵל means _____.

עַמְּךָ means "Your people" or "Your nation."

In שָׁלוֹם רָב, עַמְּךָ appears _____ time(s) and עַמּוֹ (God's people) appears _____ time(s).

🪧 PRAYER VARIATIONS

Some congregations add the phrases וְאֶת־כָּל־הָעַמִּים ("and all peoples") and וְעַל כָּל־יוֹשְׁבֵי תֵבֵל ("and upon all who live on the earth") when they ask God to bless the people of Israel with peace. Whether or not we add this phrase, we all recognize that the prayer asks for peace not just for the people of Israel, but for all the people of the world.

What is one thing you can do to bring greater peace to your friends?

בִּרְכַּת שָׁלוֹם

שִׂים שָׁלוֹם

If another student says something mean to you, how does it make you feel?

When we recite שִׂים שָׁלוֹם we ask for peace, and for a world where people are never mean, but act only with kindness and compassion.

It's easy to understand how people being nice to you can give you peace. Do you think if you are nice to others it can also bring you peace? Why or why not?

PRAYER
Practice reading שִׂים שָׁלוֹם aloud:

Grant peace (in the world), goodness	שִׂים שָׁלוֹם (בָּעוֹלָם), טוֹבָה 1
and blessing, graciousness and kindness	וּבְרָכָה, חֵן וָחֶסֶד 2
and mercy (compassion) upon us	וְרַחֲמִים עָלֵינוּ 3
and upon all Israel Your people.	וְעַל כָּל יִשְׂרָאֵל עַמֶּךָ. 4
Bless us, our Parent/Creator,	בָּרְכֵנוּ, אָבִינוּ/יוֹצְרֵנוּ, 5
all of us as one,	כֻּלָּנוּ כְּאֶחָד, 6
with the light of Your face,	בְּאוֹר פָּנֶיךָ, 7
for with the light of Your face,	כִּי בְאוֹר פָּנֶיךָ נָתַתָּ לָּנוּ, 8
Adonai our God,	יְיָ אֱלֹהֵינוּ, 9
You gave us the Torah of life,	תּוֹרַת חַיִּים, 10
and a love of kindness,	וְאַהֲבַת חֶסֶד, 11
and righteousness and blessing	וּצְדָקָה וּבְרָכָה 12
and mercy (compassion) and life and peace.	וְרַחֲמִים, וְחַיִּים וְשָׁלוֹם. 13
And may it be good in Your eyes to bless	וְטוֹב בְּעֵינֶיךָ לְבָרֵךְ 14
Your people Israel (and all peoples)	אֶת עַמְּךָ יִשְׂרָאֵל (וְאֶת-כָּל-הָעַמִּים) 15
at every time and at every hour.	בְּכָל-עֵת וּבְכָל-שָׁעָה 16
with Your peace.	בִּשְׁלוֹמֶךָ. 17
Praised are You, Adonai,	בָּרוּךְ אַתָּה, יְיָ, 18
who blesses God's people Israel with peace.	הַמְבָרֵךְ אֶת עַמּוֹ יִשְׂרָאֵל בַּשָּׁלוֹם. 19

PRAYER DICTIONARY

שִׂים
grant, put

טוֹבָה
goodness

חֵן
graciousness

אָבִינוּ
our parent

כֻּלָּנוּ כְּאֶחָד
all of us as one

נָתַתָּ
you gave

תּוֹרַת חַיִּים
Torah of life

וְאַהֲבַת חֶסֶד
and a love of kindness

א פ ג PRAYER BUILDING BLOCKS
שִׂים שָׁלוֹם "grant peace"

The root of שִׂים is שׂימ. The root שׂימ tells us that "grant" or "put" is part of a word's meaning.

In שָׁלוֹם רָב on page 54, (circle) the word with the root שׂימ.

Now, look at שִׂים שָׁלוֹם on page 56 and (circle) all the words having to do with peace. How many words did you circle?_____

Both שָׁלוֹם רָב and שִׂים שָׁלוֹם ask God to grant us peace. How else are these prayers similar?

ASKING FAVORS

שִׂים שָׁלוֹם asks God to bless us with six favors, or gifts.

Below are the English meanings of the six gifts we ask of God. Write each one in the blank space next to its matching Hebrew word.

blessing   kindness   peace   goodness   mercy   graciousness

4 חֵן _____   1 שָׁלוֹם _____

5 חֶסֶד _____   2 טוֹבָה _____

6 רַחֲמִים _____   3 בְּרָכָה _____

Which of the six gifts do you consider to be the most important? Why?

✝ PRAYER VARIATIONS

Just as some congregations add the phrase וְאֶת-כָּל-הָעַמִּים ("and all peoples") to the prayer for peace, so too, others add the word בָּעוֹלָם ("in the world"), to indicate that our wish is for peace for everyone. Some congregations call God אָבִינוּ ("our Parent"), while others call God יוֹצְרֵנוּ ("our Creator").

Does your congregation include these variations?

בִּרְכַּת שָׁלוֹם

בָּרְכֵנוּ, אָבִינוּ "bless us, our Parent"

Write the root of בָּרְכֵנוּ. ___ ___ ___

What does this root mean?_____

אָבִינוּ literally means "our father."
Because God is neither male nor female—not father or mother—many choose to translate אָבִינוּ as "our Parent."

Read each of the sentences below aloud, then (circle) the word that means "our Parent."

1 אָבִינוּ מַלְכֵּנוּ, חָנֵּנוּ וַעֲנֵנוּ, כִּי אֵין בָּנוּ מַעֲשִׂים.

2 אָבִינוּ הָאָב הָרַחֲמָן, הַמְרַחֵם, רַחֵם עָלֵינוּ.

3 סְלַח לָנוּ אָבִינוּ כִּי חָטָאנוּ.

Why do you think we call God our Parent? Why not our brother, sister, president, or boss?

_____

FROM THE TEXT

The quest for peace—שָׁלוֹם—has always been important to the Jewish people.

Read the following biblical verse from the prophet Isaiah. *(Isaiah 2:4)*

**And they shall beat their swords into plowshares and their spears into pruning-hooks;
Nation shall not lift up sword against nation, neither shall they learn war any more.**

Now read the Hebrew for the second half of the verse.

לֹא־יִשָּׂא גוֹי אֶל־גּוֹי חֶרֶב וְלֹא־יִלְמְדוּ עוֹד מִלְחָמָה...

Isaiah lived more than 2,500 years ago. Why are his words still meaningful to us today?

_____

WHERE WE ARE

Look ahead to page 94 and find שִׂים שָׁלוֹם.

On Shabbat morning, שִׂים שָׁלוֹם comes right after the _____

and before _____ .

עֹשֶׂה שָׁלוֹם

עֹשֶׂה
makes

יַעֲשֶׂה
(will) make

עָלֵינוּ
for us, on us

וְעַל
and for, and on

כָּל
all

וְאִמְרוּ
and say

אָמֵן
Amen

There are so many kinds of שָׁלוֹם that we want—peace among countries, among family members, and among friends. The prayer בִּרְכַּת עֹשֶׂה שָׁלוֹם ("make peace") is said immediately after and asks God to make peace in our lives and world.

PRAYER
Practice reading עֹשֶׂה שָׁלוֹם aloud:

1	עֹשֶׂה שָׁלוֹם
	May God who makes peace
2	בִּמְרוֹמָיו,
	in the heavens
3	הוּא יַעֲשֶׂה שָׁלוֹם עָלֵינוּ,
	make peace for us,
4	וְעַל כָּל־יִשְׂרָאֵל,
	and for all Israel,
5	(וְעַל כָּל־יוֹשְׁבֵי תֵבֵל).
	(and for all who live on the earth).
6	וְאִמְרוּ, אָמֵן.
	And say, Amen.

THE ROOT עשׂה

The root of עֹשֶׂה and יַעֲשֶׂה is עשׂה. עשׂה means "make."

Circle the root letters in each word below.

לְמַעֲשֶׂה   עֹשֶׂה   יַעֲשֶׂה   שֶׁעָשָׂה

PRAYER IN MOTION
Look ahead on page 87 to see that עֹשֶׂה שָׁלוֹם also appears at the end of the Kaddish (קַדִּישׁ). In many congregations it is traditional to take three steps backward, to bow to the left, the right, and the center when saying עֹשֶׂה שָׁלוֹם. It is as if we are bowing before the Ruler. What is your own reaction to bowing?

PRAYER VARIATIONS
Some congregations add the phrase וְעַל כָּל־יוֹשְׁבֵי תֵבֵל ("and upon all who live on the earth") when they ask God to bless the people with peace. Does your congregation add this phrase?

בִּרְכַּת שָׁלוֹם

אֵין כָּמוֹךָ

When you get a present you really, really want, how do you like to show appreciation? Do you say, "Thanks!" or give a big hug?

The Torah is one of the greatest gifts received by the Jewish people. Before we read from the Torah, the congregation says thank you for the Torah by praising God. For example, when we say אֵין כָּמוֹךָ, we are saying that there are no other gods as great as Adonai.

Most congregations read a portion of the Torah on Shabbat morning. The Torah service has three parts: 1) taking the Torah out of the Ark, 2) reading the Torah, and 3) returning the Torah to the Ark. Each part of the Torah service has its own prayers and blessings.

When is the Torah read in your congregation?

 PRAYER

Practice reading אֵין כָּמוֹךָ aloud:

1	אֵין כָּמוֹךָ,	There is none like You, Adonai,
2	בָאֱלֹהִים, יְיָ,	among the gods (other people worship),
3	וְאֵין כְּמַעֲשֶׂיךָ.	and there are no deeds like Yours.
4	מַלְכוּתְךָ מַלְכוּת	Your sovereignty is
5	כָּל עֹלָמִים,	an eternal sovereignty,
6	וּמֶמְשַׁלְתְּךָ	and Your reign
7	בְּכָל דּוֹר וָדֹר.	is from generation to generation.
8	יְיָ מֶלֶךְ, יְיָ מָלָךְ,	Adonai is Ruler, Adonai ruled,
9	יְיָ יִמְלֹךְ לְעוֹלָם וָעֶד.	Adonai will rule forever and ever.
10	יְיָ עֹז לְעַמּוֹ יִתֵּן,	May Adonai give strength to God's people,
11	יְיָ יְבָרֵךְ אֶת־עַמּוֹ בַשָּׁלוֹם.	May Adonai bless God's people with peace.

PRAYER DICTIONARY

אֵין
(there is) none

כָּמוֹךָ
like You

(כְּ)מַעֲשֶׂיךָ
(like) Your deeds

מַלְכוּתְךָ
Your sovereignty

וּמֶמְשַׁלְתְּךָ
and Your reign

מֶלֶךְ
(is) ruler

מָלָךְ
ruled

יִמְלֹךְ
will rule

PAST, PRESENT, FUTURE

The root מלכ tells us that "king" or "ruler" is part of a word's meaning. Each word next to יְיָ below is built on the root מלכ.

Write whether the words below are in the past, present, or future tense.

Tense	
_____	יְיָ מָלָךְ
_____	יְיָ יִמְלֹךְ
_____	יְיָ מֶלֶךְ

FROM THE TEXT

The prayer phrase יְיָ מֶלֶךְ, יְיָ מָלָךְ, יְיָ יִמְלֹךְ לְעֹלָם וָעֶד is a compilation of verses from different parts of the Bible.

Read each biblical verse below and (circle) the phrase that appears in אֵין כָּמוֹךָ. *(Remember: God's name can be written as* יְהֹוָה *or* יְיָ*.)*

Psalm 10:16 …יְהֹוָה מֶלֶךְ עוֹלָם וָעֶד אָבְדוּ גוֹיִם מֵאַרְצוֹ

Psalm 96:10 ……אִמְרוּ בַגּוֹיִם יְהֹוָה מָלָךְ אַף־תִּכּוֹן תֵּבֵל בַּל־תִּמּוֹט יָדִין עַמִּים בְּמֵישָׁרִים:

Exodus 15:18 ……………יְהֹוָה יִמְלֹךְ לְעֹלָם וָעֶד:

There is no single verse in the Bible that says God is, was, and will always be Ruler, yet the prayer expresses all these ideas in one sentence. Why do you think the prayer combines all these thoughts?

_____

_____

_____

אֵין כָּמוֹךָ/אַב הָרַחֲמִים/כִּי מִצִּיּוֹן/לְךָ יְיָ

אַב הָרַחֲמִים

Whom do you trust? Your friends? Your parents? Why do you trust them?

In אַב הָרַחֲמִים, we announce that we trust God, and ask God to protect Jerusalem. It is the second prayer recited as the Ark is opened for the Torah service.

Why do you think in this prayer that focuses on trust, we choose to call God אָב—Parent—as opposed to מֶלֶךְ—Ruler?

PRAYER

Practice reading אַב הָרַחֲמִים aloud:

Merciful Parent,	אַב הָרַחֲמִים, 1
favor Zion with Your goodness;	הֵיטִיבָה בִרְצוֹנְךָ אֶת־צִיּוֹן; 2
rebuild the walls of Jerusalem.	תִּבְנֶה חוֹמוֹת יְרוּשָׁלָיִם. 3
For in You alone do we trust,	כִּי בְךָ לְבַד בָּטָחְנוּ, 4
sovereign God, high and exalted,	מֶלֶךְ אֵל רָם וְנִשָּׂא, 5
eternal Ruler.	אֲדוֹן עוֹלָמִים. 6

TORAH READING

After the destruction of the First Temple, some of the Jews who had been exiled were allowed to return to Israel. When they returned, their leader, Ezra the Scribe, was determined to rebuild Jewish life and Torah law.

Ezra knew the people would have to be reminded of the meaning of the Torah, so he arranged for public Torah readings to take place every Monday, Thursday, Shabbat, and on certain holidays. To this day—thousands of years later—many congregations still read from the Torah in the synagogue at these same times.

Do you think it is still important today that we read from the Torah every week? Why or why not?

_____

_____

הָרַחֲמִים
*merciful,
the mercy*

יְרוּשָׁלַיִם
Jerusalem

בָּטָחְנוּ
we trust(ed)

ROOTS

The root רחם means "mercy" or "compassion." The three letters רחם tell us that "mercy" or "compassion" is part of a word's meaning.

In this prayer, we call God אַב הָרַחֲמִים ("merciful Parent"). God is sometimes referred to by three other names, all expressing the idea that God is compassionate. Those names are:

God full of mercy .... אֵל מָלֵא רַחֲמִים

the merciful one .... הָרַחֲמָן

compassionate and gracious God .... אֵל רַחוּם וְחַנּוּן

Read each of the above names for God aloud. Then (circle) the root letters רחם in each of the names.

ZION AND JERUSALEM

אַב הָרַחֲמִים asks God to favor Zion צִיּוֹן (Jerusalem) with goodness and to rebuild it. הַתִּקְוָה, Israel's national anthem, also speaks of Zion and Jerusalem.

Underline יְרוּשָׁלַיִם and צִיּוֹן wherever they appear in the words of הַתִּקְוָה, below:

Within the heart .... כָּל עוֹד בַּלֵּבָב פְּנִימָה

a Jewish spirit is still alive .... נֶפֶשׁ יְהוּדִי הוֹמִיָּה

and the eyes look eastward .... וּלְפַאֲתֵי מִזְרָח קָדִימָה

toward Zion. .... עַיִן לְצִיּוֹן צוֹפִיָּה

Our hope is not lost, ... עוֹד לֹא אָבְדָה תִקְוָתֵנוּ

the hope of two thousand years .... הַתִּקְוָה בַּת שְׁנוֹת אַלְפַּיִם

to be a free nation in our land, ... לִהְיוֹת עַם חָפְשִׁי בְּאַרְצֵנוּ

the land of Zion and Jerusalem .... אֶרֶץ צִיּוֹן וִירוּשָׁלָיִם

אֵין כָּמוֹךָ/אַב הָרַחֲמִים/כִּי מִצִּיּוֹן/לְךָ יְיָ

כִּי מִצִּיּוֹן

What links you to your past? To your future? Perhaps you have a gift from a grandparent that connects you to them. In the same way, the Torah links us to our ancestors and to our descendants. The teachings of the Torah are passed down as we read from it each week.

The prayer that we say as we remove the Torah from the Ark, כִּי מִצִּיּוֹן, expresses our hope and our belief that both the Torah and the land of Israel will continue to be a source of strength for our children and grandchildren.

What is a favorite story or teaching of yours from the Torah that you would like to pass down to the next generation?

PRAYER

Practice reading כִּי מִצִּיּוֹן aloud:

For out of Zion shall go forth Torah,	כִּי מִצִּיּוֹן תֵּצֵא תוֹרָה,	1
and the word of God from Jerusalem.	וּדְבַר־יְיָ מִירוּשָׁלָיִם.	2
Praised is the One, who gave the Torah	בָּרוּךְ שֶׁנָּתַן תּוֹרָה	3
to God's people Israel in holiness.	לְעַמּוֹ יִשְׂרָאֵל בִּקְדֻשָּׁתוֹ.	4

PRAYER VARIATIONS

As the Ark is opened, some congregations add the following words from the Torah (*Numbers 10:35*) before כִּי מִצִּיּוֹן.

When the Ark was carried forth, Moses said:	וַיְהִי בִּנְסֹעַ הָאָרֹן וַיֹּאמֶר מֹשֶׁה,	5
Arise, Adonai; may Your enemies be scattered,	קוּמָה, יְיָ, וְיָפֻצוּ אֹיְבֶיךָ,	6
may Your foes be driven to flight.	וְיָנֻסוּ מְשַׂנְאֶיךָ מִפָּנֶיךָ.	7

מִצִּיוֹן
from Zion

תּוֹרָה
Torah, teaching

וּדְבַר
and the word of

מִירוּשָׁלָיִם
from Jerusalem

שֶׁנָּתַן
who gave

לְעַמּוֹ
to God's people

בִּקְדֻשָּׁתוֹ
in God's holiness

Other congregations do not mention war or the Jews' enemies, but add:

8 הָבוּ גֹדֶל לֵאלֹהֵינוּ............... *Let us declare God's greatness*

9 וּתְנוּ כָבוֹד לַתּוֹרָה............... *and give honor to the Torah.*

No matter which words they add before כִּי מִצִּיוֹן, all congregations are alike in praising God for giving us the Torah. Which version of the prayer does your congregation recite?

BUILDING YOUR VOCABULARY

Study the Prayer Dictionary. Then cover it and draw a line from each Hebrew word to its English meaning below.

to God's people	תּוֹרָה
from Zion	וּדְבַר
and the word of	מִירוּשָׁלָיִם
from Jerusalem	מִצִּיוֹן
in God's holiness	שֶׁנָּתַן
who gave	לְעַמּוֹ
Torah, teaching	בִּקְדֻשָּׁתוֹ

PRAYER IN MOTION

As we recite כִּי מִצִּיוֹן the Ark is opened and the congregation rises. It is traditional to stand whenever the Ark is open or when someone is carrying a Torah. Why do you think we stand on these occasions?

_____

WHERE WE ARE

Look ahead to page 94 and find אֵין כָּמוֹךָ, אַב הָרַחֲמִים, לְךָ יְיָ, and כִּי מִצִּיוֹן.

On Shabbat morning, these prayers come right after _____

and before _____ .

אֵין כָּמוֹךָ/אַב הָרַחֲמִים/כִּי מִצִּיוֹן/לְךָ יְיָ

HOLDING THE TORAH

In many congregations, the person holding the Torah after it is taken out of the Ark recites each of the following lines, first alone, and then with the congregation. In other congregations, the lines are recited in unison.

Hear O Israel:		שְׁמַע יִשְׂרָאֵל: 1
Adonai is our God, Adonai is One.		יְיָ אֱלֹהֵינוּ, יְיָ אֶחָד. 2
Our God is One and is great;		אֶחָד אֱלֹהֵינוּ, גָּדוֹל אֲדוֹנֵנוּ, 3
God's name is holy.		קָדוֹשׁ שְׁמוֹ. 4

In some congregations, the person holding the Torah turns to face the Ark. The leader and the congregation bow when reciting the opening words גַּדְּלוּ לַייָ.

Acclaim Adonai with me,		גַּדְּלוּ לַייָ אִתִּי, 5
and together let us exalt God's name.		וּנְרוֹמְמָה שְׁמוֹ יַחְדָּו. 6

When you become a Bar or Bat Mitzvah you will most likely have the honor of holding the Torah when it is taken from the Ark.

How do you think you might feel when holding the Torah?

לְךָ יְיָ

Traditionally, after the Torah is removed from the Ark, we stand as the Torah is carried up and down the aisles, from the Ark to the bimah. During this procession, we sing לְךָ יְיָ, a prayer that praises God's greatness. Why do you think we carry the Torah up and down the aisles, among the congregation, before we read from it?

Practice reading לְךָ יְיָ *aloud:*

Yours, God is the greatness, the power,		לְךָ, יְיָ, הַגְּדֻלָּה וְהַגְּבוּרָה, 1
the glory, the victory, and the majesty;		וְהַתִּפְאֶרֶת וְהַנֵּצַח וְהַהוֹד, 2
for all that is in heaven and earth,		כִּי כֹל בַּשָּׁמַיִם וּבָאָרֶץ, 3
is Yours. Yours is the sovereignty, God;		לְךָ יְיָ הַמַּמְלָכָה: 4
You are supreme over all.		וְהַמִּתְנַשֵּׂא לְכֹל לְרֹאשׁ. 5

בִּרְכוֹת הַתּוֹרָה

Did you know that if you go to synagogue this Shabbat, you will be hearing the same Torah portion as Jews in Tokyo, London, and San Francisco? Each week, the same Torah portion—פָּרָשָׁה—is read throughout the world.

Each פָּרָשָׁה is divided into sections, or readings. As each section is read, one or more congregants are called up to the Torah to say two blessings—one before the Torah reader begins to read that section, and one after the reader has finished. The honor of being called up to recite these blessings is called an עֲלִיָּה ("going up").

The blessing before the Torah reading has two parts. The first part is the בָּרְכוּ, a call to the congregation to praise God. The second part thanks God for choosing us to receive the gift of the Torah.

What is another time that we recite the בָּרְכוּ? *(Hint: Look back at chapter 3.)*

BLESSING BEFORE THE TORAH READING
Practice reading the blessing aloud:

(The leader chants:)

Praise Adonai, who is to be praised. .... בָּרְכוּ אֶת־יְיָ הַמְבֹרָךְ. 1

(The congregation responds:)

Praised is Adonai, who is to be praised .... בָּרוּךְ יְיָ הַמְבֹרָךְ 2

forever and ever. .... לְעוֹלָם וָעֶד. 3

(The leader repeats lines 2 and 3, and then continues)

Praised are You, Adonai our God, ... בָּרוּךְ אַתָּה, יְיָ אֱלֹהֵינוּ, 4

Ruler of the world, ... מֶלֶךְ הָעוֹלָם, 5

for choosing us from all the nations .... אֲשֶׁר בָּחַר־בָּנוּ מִכָּל־הָעַמִּים 6

and giving us God's Torah. .... וְנָתַן־לָנוּ אֶת־תּוֹרָתוֹ. 7

Praised are You, Adonai, who gives us the Torah. .... בָּרוּךְ אַתָּה, יְיָ, נוֹתֵן הַתּוֹרָה. 8

ROOTS

The root נתן means "give." The three letters נתן tell us that "give" is part of a word's meaning.

(Circle) the root letters in each word. Then write its English meaning.

נוֹתֵן _____

נָתַן _____

א פ ג PRAYER BUILDING BLOCKS

אֲשֶׁר בָּחַר־בָּנוּ "who chose us" ("for choosing us")

אֲשֶׁר means "who."

בָּחַר means "chose."

בָּנוּ means "us."

To whom do you think "us" refers?

Some people explain that this means God chose the Jews for special responsibilities. What do you think those responsibilities might be?

_____

_____

PRAYER VARIATIONS

In place of the phrase אֲשֶׁר בָּחַר־בָּנוּ מִכָּל־הָעַמִּים, Reconstructionist prayer books use the phrase אֲשֶׁר קֵרְבָנוּ לַעֲבוֹדָתוֹ "who has drawn us to Your service." Whether we praise God for drawing us near to God's service or for choosing us from the nations, we all praise God for giving us the Torah.

Which phrase is in your congregation's prayer book?

_____

PRAYER DICTIONARY

בָּחַר
chose (choosing)

בָּנוּ
us

מִכָּל
from all

הָעַמִּים
the nations

וְנָתַן
and gave (and giving)

לָנוּ
to us

תּוֹרָתוֹ
God's Torah

נוֹתֵן
gives

A Yad, pointer, used for reading the Torah

BLESSING AFTER THE TORAH READING

The blessing recited after the Torah reading praises God for giving us the Torah of truth and eternal life. By reading the Torah and passing its lessons down to our children and then to their children, we can keep our heritage alive forever. The chain of tradition that began when the Israelites received the Torah almost 3,500 years ago lives on as we hear its words each week.

3,500 years is a long time! Can you think of anything else that is that old and goes back that far?

PRAYER
Practice reading the blessing aloud:

1	בָּרוּךְ אַתָּה, יְיָ אֱלֹהֵינוּ,
Praised are You, Adonai our God,	
2	מֶלֶךְ הָעוֹלָם,
Ruler of the world,	
3	אֲשֶׁר נָתַן־לָנוּ תּוֹרַת אֱמֶת,
who gave us the Torah of truth,	
4	וְחַיֵּי עוֹלָם נָטַע בְּתוֹכֵנוּ.
and implanted within us eternal life.	
5	בָּרוּךְ אַתָּה, יְיָ, נוֹתֵן הַתּוֹרָה.
Praised are You, Adonai, who gives us the Torah.	

PRAYER IN MOTION

We are careful not to touch a Torah scroll directly, because the natural oils in our hands can damage the ink and parchment. But we still want to note the place where we are reading from and keep track of which part we are up to. The reader uses a pointer, a יָד, instead of a finger to follow along in the text. And, in many synagogues, the one honored with the aliyah holds a siddur, the end of a tallit, or the Torah binder and uses it to touch the words of the Torah that are about to be read. After they touch the words with the object, a person will kiss the object that has touched the words of Torah, then take hold of the Torah's handles and recite the Torah blessing.

Why do you think some people kiss the item that touched the Torah's words?

בְּרְכוֹת הַתּוֹרָה/בִּרְכוֹת הַהַפְטָרָה

BUILDING YOUR VOCABULARY

Read each of the Hebrew phrases aloud.

Connect each Hebrew phrase to its English meaning.

Then put a check next to the phrases that have "world" or "eternal" as part of their meaning.

and eternal life   ___   לְעוֹלָם וָעֶד

ruler of the world   ___   תּוֹרַת אֱמֶת

forever and ever   ___   וְחַיֵּי עוֹלָם

Torah of truth   ___   מֶלֶךְ הָעוֹלָם

PRAYER DICTIONARY

תּוֹרַת
Torah of

אֱמֶת
truth

וְחַיֵּי
and life (of)

עוֹלָם
eternal, world

ALIYAH

Why do we use the term עֲלִיָּה ("going up") for reciting the Torah blessings? We go up to the bimah when we are called to recite the blessings before and after each section of the Torah reading. We also go up in the eyes of the congregation when we receive this honor. And many people feel they go up, or move spiritually closer, to God.

You may have heard the word עֲלִיָּה in a different context. Going to live in Israel is called עֲלִיָּה (we "make aliyah"). We don't just move to the Holy Land, we go up to it.

The number of עֲלִיּוֹת during a Torah reading depends on when the reading takes place. For example, on Mondays and Thursdays there are three עֲלִיּוֹת, on Yom Kippur there are six, and on Shabbat morning there are usually seven. The number of עֲלִיּוֹת indicates the level of holiness of the day.

Based on the number of עֲלִיּוֹת on the different days, what is the holiest day in the Jewish calendar?

_____

בִּרְכוֹת הַהַפְטָרָה

When you become a Bar or Bat Mitzvah and are called up to the Torah for the first time, you might be the one to chant the haftarah, הַפְטָרָה ("conclusion"), that day. The הַפְטָרָה is a passage from the Book of Prophets. It is often related by theme to that week's Torah portion.

Both the Torah and the הַפְטָרָה are chanted according to musical notations (trope) shown by markings under and over the words themselves. The tunes of the trope for the Torah and הַפְטָרָה differ slightly from one another.

Read this verse from the Torah and (circle) the trope marks:
(Hint: Look for marks above and below the letters that are not vowels.)

זָכוֹר אֶת־יוֹם הַשַּׁבָּת לְקַדְּשׁוֹ:

Below is the blessing recited before the haftarah is read. (Circle) two lines that you find most interesting. What do you find interesting about those lines?

BLESSING BEFORE THE HAFTARAH READING

Practice reading the blessing aloud:

Praised are You, Adonai our God,	1 בָּרוּךְ אַתָּה, יְיָ אֱלֹהֵינוּ,
Ruler of the world,	2 מֶלֶךְ הָעוֹלָם,
who chose good (faithful) prophets,	3 אֲשֶׁר בָּחַר בִּנְבִיאִים טוֹבִים,
and was pleased with their words	4 וְרָצָה בְדִבְרֵיהֶם הַנֶּאֱמָרִים
spoken in truth. Praised are You, Adonai,	5 בֶּאֱמֶת. בָּרוּךְ אַתָּה יְיָ,
the One who takes delight in (chooses) the Torah,	6 הַבּוֹחֵר בַּתּוֹרָה,
and in Moses, God's servant,	7 וּבְמֹשֶׁה עַבְדּוֹ,
and in Israel, God's people,	8 וּבְיִשְׂרָאֵל עַמּוֹ,
and in the prophets of truth and righteousness (justice).	9 וּבִנְבִיאֵי הָאֱמֶת וָצֶדֶק.

THE FAMILY CONNECTION

There are three sets of related words in the blessing before the הַפְטָרָה reading.

1	2	3
בָּחַר	בִּנְבִיאִים	בֶּאֱמֶת
הַבּוֹחֵר	וּבִנְבִיאֵי	הָאֱמֶת

Write the number that goes with each word pair next to its English meaning.

_____ prophets _____ choose _____ truth

FROM THE TEXT

Pirkei Avot, a section of the Mishnah compiled by the rabbis about 1700 years ago, begins with this teaching:

מֹשֶׁה קִבֵּל תּוֹרָה מִסִּינַי, וּמְסָרָהּ לִיהוֹשֻׁעַ,
וִיהוֹשֻׁעַ לִזְקֵנִים, וּזְקֵנִים לִנְבִיאִים...

Moses received the Torah at Sinai, and he transmitted it to Joshua, and Joshua to the Elders, and the Elders to the Prophets...
(Pirkei Avot 1:1)

Find and underline the Hebrew word for Prophets in Pirkei Avot 1:1.

What are some things you learn about the Prophets from this teaching?

_____

WHERE WE ARE

Look ahead to page 94 and find בִּרְכוֹת הַהַפְטָרָה.

On Shabbat morning, these blessings come right after and before _____ .

PRAYER DICTIONARY

בָּחַר
chose (choosing)

בִּנְבִיאִים
prophets

טוֹבִים
good (faithful)

הַנֶּאֱמָרִים
spoken

בֶּאֱמֶת
in truth

הַבּוֹחֵר
the one who chooses

עַבְדּוֹ
God's servant

עַמּוֹ
God's people

וְצֶדֶק
and righteousness (justice)

Mountains in the Sinai desert

BLESSINGS AFTER THE HAFTARAH READING

We say the four blessings below after the haftarah reading. Read the first blessing, and (circle) two lines from it which you find most interesting.

What do you find interesting about these lines?

_____

_____

 PRAYER

Practice reading the first blessing after the haftarah aloud:

I.

Praised are You, Adonai our God,	בָּרוּךְ אַתָּה, יְיָ אֱלֹהֵינוּ,	1
Ruler of the world, rock of all eternity,	מֶלֶךְ הָעוֹלָם, צוּר כָּל הָעוֹלָמִים,	2
righteous in all generations,	צַדִּיק בְּכָל הַדּוֹרוֹת,	3
the faithful God, the One who says and does,	הָאֵל הַנֶּאֱמָן הָאוֹמֵר וְעֹשֶׂה,	4
the One who speaks and fulfills,	הַמְדַבֵּר וּמְקַיֵּם,	5
for all God's words are truthful and just.	שֶׁכָּל־דְּבָרָיו אֱמֶת וָצֶדֶק.	6
You are faithful, Adonai our God,	נֶאֱמָן אַתָּה הוּא, יְיָ אֱלֹהֵינוּ,	7
and faithful are Your words, and not one	וְנֶאֱמָנִים דְּבָרֶיךָ, וְדָבָר אֶחָד	8
of Your words will return empty;	מִדְּבָרֶיךָ אָחוֹר לֹא יָשׁוּב רֵיקָם,	9
For You are a faithful and compassionate	כִּי אֵל מֶלֶךְ נֶאֱמָן	10
God and Ruler. Praised are You,	וְרַחֲמָן אָתָּה. בָּרוּךְ אַתָּה,	11
Adonai, faithful in all Your words.	יְיָ, הָאֵל הַנֶּאֱמָן בְּכָל־דְּבָרָיו.	12

 73

בִּרְכוֹת הַתּוֹרָה/בִּרְכוֹת הַהַפְטָרָה

Practice reading blessings II, III and IV, which are said after the haftarah reading.

Blessing II asks God to have mercy on and to protect Zion, and prays for our return there. In ancient times, Zion was another name for Jerusalem.

II.

1 רַחֵם עַל־צִיּוֹן כִּי הִיא בֵּית חַיֵּינוּ,

2 וְלַעֲלוּבַת נֶפֶשׁ תּוֹשִׁיעַ בִּמְהֵרָה בְיָמֵינוּ.

3 בָּרוּךְ אַתָּה, יְיָ, מְשַׂמֵּחַ צִיּוֹן בְּבָנֶיהָ.

Blessing III asks God to reinstate the descendants of David as the rulers of the Jewish people.

III.

4 שַׂמְּחֵנוּ, יְיָ אֱלֹהֵינוּ, בְּאֵלִיָּהוּ הַנָּבִיא עַבְדֶּךָ,

5 וּבְמַלְכוּת בֵּית דָּוִד מְשִׁיחֶךָ, בִּמְהֵרָה יָבֹא וְיָגֵל לִבֵּנוּ.

6 עַל־כִּסְאוֹ לֹא־יֵשֵׁב זָר וְלֹא־יִנְחֲלוּ עוֹד אֲחֵרִים אֶת־כְּבוֹדוֹ,

7 כִּי בְשֵׁם קָדְשְׁךָ נִשְׁבַּעְתָּ לּוֹ שֶׁלֹּא־יִכְבֶּה נֵרוֹ לְעוֹלָם וָעֶד.

8 בָּרוּךְ אַתָּה, יְיָ, מָגֵן דָּוִד.

Blessing IV thanks God for (1) the Torah, (2) the worship service, (3) the prophets, and (4) Shabbat, our holy day of rest.

IV.

9 עַל־הַתּוֹרָה, וְעַל־הָעֲבוֹדָה, וְעַל־הַנְּבִיאִים,

10 וְעַל־יוֹם הַשַּׁבָּת הַזֶּה, שֶׁנָּתַתָּ־לָּנוּ,

11 יְיָ אֱלֹהֵינוּ, לִקְדֻשָּׁה וְלִמְנוּחָה, לְכָבוֹד וּלְתִפְאָרֶת,

12 עַל־הַכֹּל, יְיָ אֱלֹהֵינוּ, אֲנַחְנוּ מוֹדִים לָךְ,

13 וּמְבָרְכִים אוֹתָךְ. יִתְבָּרַךְ שִׁמְךָ בְּפִי כָּל חַי תָּמִיד לְעוֹלָם וָעֶד.

14 בָּרוּךְ אַתָּה יְיָ, מְקַדֵּשׁ הַשַּׁבָּת.

וְזֹאת הַתּוֹרָה

Have you ever gotten a really good grade on a test? Or drawn an impressive picture? Did you hold it up and show it to your parents or friends to see? In the same way, the Jewish people are proud of the Torah, and each time after it is read we lift it up high so the congregation can see it, and proclaim that these are the teachings that Moses set before the children of Israel, as given by God.

The honor of lifting up the Torah is called הַגְבָּהָה. Before returning the Torah to the Ark, we roll it closed and dress it again in its cover and ornaments. This honor is called גְּלִילָה.

You have to be strong to do הַגְבָּהָה—an average Torah weighs about 20 pounds—that's heavier than two gallon containers of water! Imagine lifting a gallon container in each hand, high over your head!

When do you think is the easiest time of the year to lift a Torah? The hardest? Why?

_____

_____

 PRAYER

Practice reading וְזֹאת הַתּוֹרָה aloud:

And this is the Torah that Moses placed.............	וְזֹאת הַתּוֹרָה אֲשֶׁר־שָׂם מֹשֶׁה 1
before the people of Israel	לִפְנֵי בְּנֵי יִשְׂרָאֵל 2
by the word of Adonai through Moses.	עַל־פִּי יְיָ בְּיַד־מֹשֶׁה. 3

 WHERE WE ARE

Look ahead to page 94 and find וְזֹאת הַתּוֹרָה. On Shabbat morning, this prayer

comes right after _____ and before _____ .

BUILDING YOUR VOCABULARY

Read all the Hebrew words aloud. Then (circle) the Hebrew word that means the same as the English.

Israel	אֲבוֹתֵינוּ	לְעוֹלָם וָעֶד	יִשְׂרָאֵל
Moses	מֹשֶׁה	מֶלֶךְ	מִצִיּוֹן
and this is	וְחַיֵּי עוֹלָם	וְזֹאת	וְנָתַן
placed, put	שָׁם	בָּחַר	עֹשֶׂה
before	לָנוּ	לְפָנֵי	בָּנוּ

PRAYER DICTIONARY

וְזֹאת
and this is

שָׁם
placed, put

מֹשֶׁה
Moses

לְפָנֵי
before

בְּנֵי
people of

יִשְׂרָאֵל
Israel

FROM THE TEXT

וְזֹאת הַתּוֹרָה is taken from these two Torah verses.

Deuteronomy 4:44 וְזֹאת הַתּוֹרָה אֲשֶׁר־שָׂם מֹשֶׁה לִפְנֵי בְּנֵי יִשְׂרָאֵל:

Numbers 9:23 אֶת־מִשְׁמֶרֶת יְהֹוָה שָׁמָרוּ עַל־פִּי יְהֹוָה בְּיַד־מֹשֶׁה:

Find and underline all the words of וְזֹאת הַתּוֹרָה in the verses. (Remember: יְיָ can also be written יְהֹוָה.)

Look back at page 75 and read the English meaning of וְזֹאת הַתּוֹרָה. Why do you think these words were chosen to be recited as we look at the Torah being held high?

עֵץ חַיִּים הִיא

Did you ever hear someone described as being as strong as an ox? Or as wise as an owl? Sometimes we use comparisons like that to illustrate an idea. עֵץ חַיִּים הִיא, the prayer that we sing as the Torah is returned to the Ark, begins with such a comparison. It describes the Torah as a tree of life. Just as a tree is a living thing, with roots that reach down into the earth and branches that reach up to the sun, the Torah's roots reach back to our ancestors who first received it and its branches are the generations that continue to read it and believe in its teachings.

What else could you compare the Torah to? Why?

_____

_____

PRAYER
Practice reading עֵץ חַיִּים הִיא aloud:

1	עֵץ־חַיִּים הִיא
2	לַמַּחֲזִיקִים בָּהּ,
3	וְתֹמְכֶיהָ מְאֻשָּׁר.
4	דְּרָכֶיהָ דַרְכֵי־נֹעַם,
5	וְכָל־נְתִיבוֹתֶיהָ שָׁלוֹם.

It (the Torah) is a tree of life 1
to those who uphold it, ... 2
and those who support it are happy. 3
Its ways are ways of pleasantness 4
and all its paths are peace. 5

WHERE WE ARE
Look ahead to page 94 and find עֵץ חַיִּים הִיא. On Shabbat morning, this prayer comes right after _____ and before _____.

וְזֹאת הַתּוֹרָה/עֵץ חַיִּים הִיא/עַל שְׁלֹשָׁה דְבָרִים

BUILDING YOUR VOCABULARY

Connect each Hebrew word to its English meaning.

pleasantness	עֵץ
its ways	מְאֻשָּׁר
ways of	דְּרָכֶיהָ
happy	דַּרְכֵי
tree	נֹעַם

Fill in the English meaning for the Hebrew words describing the Torah.

_____ מְאֻשָּׁר _____ חַיִּים

_____ שָׁלוֹם _____ נֹעַם

עֵץ
tree

חַיִּים
(of) life

מְאֻשָּׁר
happy

דְּרָכֶיהָ
its ways

דַּרְכֵי
its ways

נֹעַם
pleasantness

שָׁלוֹם
peace

עֵץ חַיִּים "a tree of life"

The two wooden rollers to which the Torah parchment is attached— are called עֲצֵי חַיִּים — (the plural of עֵץ חַיִּים) trees of life.

Why is this an appropriate name for the rollers?

_____

עַל שְׁלֹשָׁה דְבָרִים

What do you think are the three most important things you need in order to live? Is that hard to answer? Why or why not? Our tradition teaches us that the three most important things our world depends on are Torah, worship, and acts of kindness. This teaching comes from the beginning of Pirkei Avot—a section of the Mishnah compiled by the rabbis about 1700 years ago. Some congregations include עַל שְׁלֹשָׁה דְבָרִים as part of the Torah service.

Which of these three things—Torah, worship, or acts of kindness—is most important to you personally? Explain why.

_____

_____

 PRAYER

Practice reading עַל שְׁלֹשָׁה דְבָרִים aloud:

The world stands on three things:	1 עַל שְׁלֹשָׁה דְבָרִים הָעוֹלָם עוֹמֵד:
On Torah, on worship,	2 עַל הַתּוֹרָה וְעַל הָעֲבוֹדָה
and on acts of loving-kindness.	3 וְעַל גְּמִילוּת חֲסָדִים.

וְזֹאת הַתּוֹרָה/עֵץ חַיִּים הִיא/עַל שְׁלֹשָׁה דְבָרִים

According to עַל שְׁלֹשָׁה דְבָרִים the world stands on three pillars Write the English meaning above each Hebrew word below.

_____

הָעוֹלָם

גְּמִילוּת חֲסָדִים   הָעֲבוֹדָה   הַתּוֹרָה

Why do you think the rabbis described the world as standing on three things? Why not two or four?

_____

_____

הָעוֹלָם עוֹמֵד "the world stands"

עוֹמֵד ("stands") and עֲמִידָה are built on the root ___ ___ ___ .

This root tells us that "standing" is part of a word's meaning.

The עֲמִידָה has several names. Why is one of the names of this prayer the עֲמִידָה? *(Hint: Look back at page 43.)*

_____

Prayer Dictionary

עַל
on

שְׁלֹשָׁה
three

דְבָרִים
things

הָעוֹלָם
the world

עוֹמֵד
stands

הַתּוֹרָה
(the) Torah

הָעֲבוֹדָה
(the) worship

גְּמִילוּת חֲסָדִים
acts of loving-kindness

עַל הַתּוֹרָה "on the Torah"

We know that הַתּוֹרָה can mean "the Torah" or the scroll itself. But when we talk about תּוֹרָה, we are also talking about what we learn from studying the תּוֹרָה.

How can studying the תּוֹרָה teach us how to act toward God (עֲבוֹדָה) and act kindly toward other people (גְּמִילוּת חֲסָדִים)?

_____

_____

הָעֲבוֹדָה "the worship"

עֲבוֹדָה means "worship" or "service to God." According to our tradition, one way that people serve God is by performing ritual mitzvot. Here are two examples of mitzvot. Can you think of two more?

1. _Light Shabbat candles_   3. _____

2. _Eat a meal in a sukkah_   4. _____

גְּמִילוּת חֲסָדִים "acts of loving-kindness"

גְּמִילוּת חֲסָדִים are mitzvot that we do to serve other people. Listed below are two examples of גְּמִילוּת חֲסָדִים.

Can you think of two more?
(We can perform acts of גְּמִילוּת חֲסָדִים for anyone, rich or poor.)

1. Visit the sick

2. Feed the hungry

3. _____

4. _____

וְזֹאת הַתּוֹרָה/עֵץ חַיִּים הִיא/עַל שְׁלֹשָׁה דְבָרִים

Have you and a friend ever promised to stay friends forever? Have you ever pledged allegiance to the flag? If you have, then you promised to be loyal to your friend and to your country. For the Jewish people, the עָלֵינוּ is a pledge of loyalty to God. During the prayer, we bend our knees and bow to show our respect for God.

Think of something or someone you are very close with. In what way is loyalty important to that relationship?

PRAYER

Practice reading these excerpts from the עָלֵינוּ aloud:

1	עָלֵינוּ לְשַׁבֵּחַ לַאֲדוֹן הַכֹּל,	It is our duty to praise the God of all,
2	לָתֵת גְּדֻלָּה לְיוֹצֵר בְּרֵאשִׁית,	to praise the Creator of the universe,
3	שֶׁלֹּא עָשָׂנוּ כְּגוֹיֵי	who has made us to be different from the peoples
4	הָאֲרָצוֹת, וְלֹא שָׂמָנוּ	of other lands, and made us to be different
5	כְּמִשְׁפְּחוֹת הָאֲדָמָה,	from the families of the earth,
6	שֶׁלֹּא שָׂם חֶלְקֵנוּ כָּהֶם,	God has made our destiny
7	וְגֹרָלֵנוּ כְּכָל הֲמוֹנָם.	and our fortunes different.
8	וַאֲנַחְנוּ כּוֹרְעִים,	We bend the knee,
9	וּמִשְׁתַּחֲוִים וּמוֹדִים,	and bow, and give thanks,
10	לִפְנֵי מֶלֶךְ מַלְכֵי הַמְּלָכִים,	before the Ruler of rulers,
11	הַקָּדוֹשׁ בָּרוּךְ הוּא.	the Holy One, who is blessed.
12	וְנֶאֱמַר: וְהָיָה יְיָ לְמֶלֶךְ	And it is said: Adonai will rule
13	עַל־כָּל־הָאָרֶץ, בַּיּוֹם הַהוּא,	all the land. On that day,
14	יִהְיֶה יְיָ אֶחָד, וּשְׁמוֹ אֶחָד.	Adonai will be One and God's name will be One.

עָלֵינוּ
it is our duty

לְשַׁבֵּחַ
to praise

(לַ)אֲדוֹן
God

הַכֹּל
of all

וַאֲנַחְנוּ
and we

וּמוֹדִים
and thank

מֶלֶךְ מַלְכֵי
הַמְּלָכִים
Ruler of rulers

הָאָרֶץ
the land

בַּיּוֹם
הַהוּא
on that day

יִהְיֶה
will be

א ב ג PRAYER BUILDING BLOCKS

עָלֵינוּ לְשַׁבֵּחַ לַאֲדוֹן הַכֹּל "it is our duty to praise the God of all"

עָלֵינוּ לְשַׁבֵּחַ means "it is our duty to praise."

The word עָלֵינוּ, we have learned, means "on us" or "for us."

Read the following excerpt from עֹשֶׂה שָׁלוֹם.

(Circle) the word that means "on us" or "for us."

הוּא יַעֲשֶׂה שָׁלוֹם עָלֵינוּ וְעַל כָּל יִשְׂרָאֵל.

God will make peace for us and for all Israel.

But in the עָלֵינוּ, in order to make the sentence flow, we translate the word עָלֵינוּ as: "It is our duty."

PRAYER VARIATIONS

There are several versions of the עָלֵינוּ. The Reform prayer book includes four passages from which to choose. It includes the traditional עָלֵינוּ, found on page 82 of this book, along with three slightly different texts, in which lines 3–7 of the traditional עָלֵינוּ have either been omitted or adapted.

The Reconstructionist prayer book replaces lines 3–7 with the following:

who gave us the Torah of truth .... שֶׁנָּתַן לָנוּ תּוֹרַת אֱמֶת

and implanted within us eternal life .... וְחַיֵּי עוֹלָם נָטַע בְּתוֹכֵנוּ

Where else in the service do we recite these words?

No matter which version of the עָלֵינוּ we recite, we are declaring our loyalty to the one God.

וַאֲנַחְנוּ כּוֹרְעִים וּמִשְׁתַּחֲוִים וּמוֹדִים

"and we bend the knee and bow and thank God"

כּוֹרְעִים וּמִשְׁתַּחֲוִים means "bend the knee and bow."

וּמוֹדִים means "and give thanks."

Do you know the word תּוֹדָה? What does it mean?

_____

How are תּוֹדָה and מוֹדִים related? _____

PRAYER IN MOTION

It is traditional to stand for the עָלֵינוּ. When we recite this prayer, we bend our knees at the word כּוֹרְעִים, bow slightly as we say וּמִשְׁתַּחֲוִים וּמוֹדִים, and then stand straight at the word לִפְנֵי. In this way we act out the words of the prayer.

Write the name of another prayer in which we bow_____.

Why do you think we bow during these prayers?

_____

לִפְנֵי מֶלֶךְ מַלְכֵי הַמְּלָכִים "before the Ruler of rulers"

לִפְנֵי means "before." We bow down before the Ruler of rulers.

What root is in each word of מֶלֶךְ מַלְכֵי הַמְּלָכִים? ___ ___ ___

This root tells us that _____ or _____
is part of a word's meaning.

WHERE WE ARE

Look ahead to page 94 and find the עָלֵינוּ. On Shabbat morning, this prayer come

right after_____ and before _____ .

The closing words of the עָלֵינוּ come directly from Prophets, נְבִיאִים—the second part of the Bible. These words are more than 2,500 years old.

וְנֶאֱמַר: וְהָיָה יְיָ לְמֶלֶךְ עַל־כָּל־הָאָרֶץ,

בַּיּוֹם הַהוּא יִהְיֶה יְיָ אֶחָד, וּשְׁמוֹ אֶחָד.

And it is said: Adonai will rule all the land. On that day, Adonai will be One and God's name will be One. *(Zechariah 14:9)*

Write your own personal pledge of allegiance to the Torah and the Jewish people.

_____

_____

PRAYING TOGETHER

When we say the עָלֵינוּ together we are praying as a community. Many words in the עָלֵינוּ end with the suffix נוּ ("us" or "our"). Praying together as a group can give us a feeling of belonging to the congregation. We realize we are not alone in our prayers.

Circle all the words in the עָלֵינוּ on page 82 that have the suffix נוּ.

How many words did you circle?_____

Do you prefer praying together with others or by yourself? Why?

_____

The Mourner's קַדִּישׁ is a prayer that people say in memory of a family member who has passed away. Yet, it doesn't mention death or loss at all. Instead, it praises God.

Why do you think that a prayer praising God is recited in memory of a loved one?

PRAYER

Practice reading the Mourner's Kaddish aloud:

1	יִתְגַּדַּל וְיִתְקַדַּשׁ שְׁמֵהּ רַבָּא	*May God's name be great and may it be made holy*
2	בְּעָלְמָא דִּי בְרָא כִרְעוּתֵהּ,	*in the world created according to God's will.*
3	וְיַמְלִיךְ מַלְכוּתֵהּ	*May God rule*
4	בְּחַיֵּיכוֹן וּבְיוֹמֵיכוֹן,	*in our own lives and our own days,*
5	וּבְחַיֵּי דְכָל בֵּית יִשְׂרָאֵל,	*and in the life of all the house of Israel,*
6	בַּעֲגָלָא וּבִזְמַן קָרִיב, וְאִמְרוּ אָמֵן.	*swiftly and soon, and say, Amen.*
7	יְהֵא שְׁמֵהּ רַבָּא מְבָרַךְ	*May God's great name be blessed*
8	לְעָלַם וּלְעָלְמֵי עָלְמַיָּא.	*forever and ever.*
9	יִתְבָּרַךְ וְיִשְׁתַּבַּח וְיִתְפָּאַר וְיִתְרוֹמַם,	*Blessed, praised, glorified, exalted,*
10	וְיִתְנַשֵּׂא וְיִתְהַדָּר וְיִתְעַלֶּה וְיִתְהַלָּל	*extolled, honored, magnified, and adored*
11	שְׁמֵהּ דְּקֻדְשָׁא, בְּרִיךְ הוּא,	*be the name of the Holy One, blessed is God.*
12	לְעֵלָּא מִן כָּל בִּרְכָתָא וְשִׁירָתָא,	*Though God is beyond all the blessings, songs,*
13	תֻּשְׁבְּחָתָא וְנֶחֱמָתָא, דַּאֲמִירָן	*adorations, and consolations that are spoken*
14	בְּעָלְמָא, וְאִמְרוּ אָמֵן.	*in the world, and say, Amen.*
15	יְהֵא שְׁלָמָא רַבָּא מִן שְׁמַיָּא	*May there be great peace from heaven*
16	וְחַיִּים עָלֵינוּ וְעַל־כָּל יִשְׂרָאֵל,	*and life for us and for all Israel,*

קַדִּישׁ
holy

יִתְגַּדַּל
will be great

וְיִתְקַדַּשׁ
and will be holy

שְׁמֵהּ
God's name

בְּעָלְמָא
in the world

וְיַמְלִיךְ
and will rule

מַלְכוּתֵהּ
God's kingdom

	Hebrew
17	וְאִמְרוּ אָמֵן.
18	עֹשֶׂה שָׁלוֹם
19	בִּמְרוֹמָיו,
20	הוּא יַעֲשֶׂה שָׁלוֹם עָלֵינוּ
21	וְעַל־כָּל־יִשְׂרָאֵל,
22	וְאִמְרוּ אָמֵן.

and say, Amen. 17
May God who makes peace 18
in the heavens, ... 19
make peace for us 20
and for all Israel, ... 21
and say, Amen. 22

THE LANGUAGE OF PRAYER

Did you know that the קַדִּישׁ is written in Aramaic and not Hebrew? Aramaic was the language that was spoken by Jews at the time the siddur was written. It was their everyday language.

Why do you think some prayers, like the קַדִּישׁ, are in Aramaic?

_____

Do you prefer saying prayers in English or Hebrew? Why?

_____

THE HEBREW-ARAMAIC CONNECTION

Many of the words in the קַדִּישׁ are related to Hebrew words you already know. Write the number of the Hebrew word next to its related Aramaic word. *(Hint: Look for related roots.)*

ARAMAIC	HEBREW
_____ יִתְגַּדַּל	מֶלֶךְ 1
_____ בְּעָלְמָא	קִדְּשָׁנוּ 2
_____ וּבְחַיֵּי	הָעוֹלָם 3
_____ קַדִּישׁ, וְיִתְקַדַּשׁ	חַיִּים 4
_____ וְיַמְלִיךְ	בָּרוּךְ 5
_____ שְׁלָמָא	שָׁלוֹם 6
_____ בְּרִיךְ	גָּדְלֶךָ 7

קַדִּישׁ

ROOTS

Write the root for each of the Aramaic words below.

Choose any three roots and write their English meanings.

ENGLISH MEANING	ROOT	ARAMAIC WORD
_____	__ __ __	בְּרִיךְ
_____	__ __ __	מַלְכוּתֵהּ
_____	__ __ __	בִּרְכָתָא
_____	__ __ __	וְיַמְלִיךְ
_____	__ __ __	יִתְגַּדַּל
_____	__ __ __	קַדִּישׁ, וְיִתְקַדַּשׁ
_____	__ __ __	שְׁלָמָא

PRAYER DICTIONARY

וּבְחַיֵּי
and in the life of

לְעָלַם
forever

וְיִשְׁתַּבַּח
and will be praised

בְּרִיךְ
blessed

בִּרְכָתָא
blessing

שְׁלָמָא
peace

ABOUT THE KADDISH

In this chapter we have learned about the Mourner's קַדִּישׁ.
There are several other versions of the קַדִּישׁ as well. (For example,
the חֲצִי קַדִּישׁ.) The different versions of the קַדִּישׁ divide up the
service, marking the end of one section of the service and the
beginning of the next. About 800 years ago the קַדִּישׁ came to be
the prayer said by mourners.

Why do you think a prayer would appear more than once in a service?

_____

A memorial candle

WHERE WE ARE

Look ahead to page 94 and find the קַדִּישׁ. On Shabbat

morning, this prayer come right after _____

and before _____ .

PRAYER IN MOTION

We say the קַדִּישׁ only in the presence of a מִנְיָן. In some congregations, only the mourners and those observing yahrzeit—the anniversary of a loved one's death—stand as they recite the Mourner's קַדִּישׁ. In other congregations, everyone stands as a sign of support for the mourners.

Why do you think we say the קַדִּישׁ only when a מִנְיָן is present?

_____

The קַדִּישׁ, like the עֲמִידָה, concludes with עֹשֶׂה שָׁלוֹם. When we say עֹשֶׂה שָׁלוֹם at the end of the קַדִּישׁ and the עֲמִידָה, it is traditional to take three steps backward, then to bow to the left, to the right, and then forward. It is as if we are leaving the presence of a king or a queen.

Why do you think we end both of these prayers with a prayer for peace?

_____

For whom do we want peace?

_____

THE THEME OF THE PRAYER

We have learned that the Mourner's Kaddish is said in memory of someone who has died, yet it contains no mention of death.

Reread the English translation of the Kaddish on pages 86 and 87. Pay attention to the tone and mood of the prayer. Then complete the following exercise.

1. Fill in the blank by choosing the correct word.

The Kaddish is a prayer of _____ to God. (thanks/praise/request)

2. Choose four words from the English translation of the prayer that illustrate your answer to number 1.

_____ _____ _____ _____

D o you know a catchy song? Does it have a set of words that repeat? At the end of the service, we sing אֵין כֵּאלֹהֵינוּ, which also has words that repeat several times.

What are your favorite songs? What mood do they put you in when you hear them?

📖 PRAYER

Practice reading these excerpts from the אֵין כֵּאלֹהֵינוּ aloud:

1	There is none like our God,	אֵין כֵּאלֹהֵינוּ,
2	There is none like our Sovereign,	אֵין כַּאדוֹנֵינוּ,
3	There is none like our Ruler,	אֵין כְּמַלְכֵּנוּ,
4	There is none like our Savior.	אֵין כְּמוֹשִׁיעֵנוּ.
5	Who is like our God? Who is like our Sovereign?	מִי כֵאלֹהֵינוּ? מִי כַאדוֹנֵינוּ?
6	Who is like our Ruler? Who is like our Savior?	מִי כְמַלְכֵּנוּ? מִי כְמוֹשִׁיעֵנוּ?
7	We will give thanks to our God,	נוֹדֶה לֵאלֹהֵינוּ,
8	We will give thanks to our Sovereign,	נוֹדֶה לַאדוֹנֵינוּ,
9	We will give thanks to our Ruler,	נוֹדֶה לְמַלְכֵּנוּ,
10	We will give thanks to our Savior.	נוֹדֶה לְמוֹשִׁיעֵנוּ.
11	Blessed is our God, Blessed is our Sovereign,	בָּרוּךְ אֱלֹהֵינוּ, בָּרוּךְ אֲדוֹנֵינוּ,
12	Blessed is our Ruler, Blessed is our Savior.	בָּרוּךְ מַלְכֵּנוּ, בָּרוּךְ מוֹשִׁיעֵנוּ.
13	You are our God,	אַתָּה הוּא אֱלֹהֵינוּ,
14	You are our Sovereign,	אַתָּה הוּא אֲדוֹנֵינוּ,
15	You are our Ruler,	אַתָּה הוּא מַלְכֵּנוּ,
16	You are our Savior.	אַתָּה הוּא מוֹשִׁיעֵנוּ.

PRAYER DICTIONARY

אֵין כְּ-
there is none like

מִי כְ-
who is like

נוֹדֶה לְ-
we will give thanks to

אַתָּה הוּא
you are

אֱלֹהֵינוּ
our God

אֲדוֹנֵינוּ
our sovereign

מַלְכֵּנוּ
our ruler

מוֹשִׁיעֵנוּ
our savior

BUILDING YOUR VOCABULARY

Read all the Hebrew words aloud. Then circle the Hebrew word that means the same as the English.

our savior	אָבִינוּ	אֱלֹהֵינוּ	מוֹשִׁיעֵנוּ
there is none like	בָּרוּךְ שֶׁ-	אֵין כְּ-	אַתָּה הוּא
our sovereign	אֲדוֹנֵינוּ	אֱלֹהֵינוּ	אֲבוֹתֵינוּ
our ruler	מַלְכֵּנוּ	קִדְּשָׁנוּ	אֱלֹהֵינוּ
we will give thanks to	בָּרְכוּ	נוֹדֶה לְ-	לְעַמּוֹ
you are	יְיָ אֶחָד	אַתָּה הוּא	עָלֵינוּ
our God	מַלְכוּתוֹ	וְצַוֵּנוּ	אֱלֹהֵינוּ
who is like	כִּי בָנוּ	נוֹדֶה לְ-	מִי כְ-

THE SECRET WORD

Read אֵין כֵּאלֹהֵינוּ on page 90. Then underline נוֹדֶה, מִי, אֵין and the first time each one appears in the hymn.

How many times does each of these appear in אֵין כֵּאלֹהֵינוּ? _____

In the spaces below, write the first letter of these three words. (Remember: כ at the end of a word is written ך)

אֵין מִי נוֹדֶה

___ ___ ___

What "secret" word did you find? When do we say this word?

_____

⬦ 91 ⬦

אֵין כֵּאלֹהֵינוּ

WORD PARTS

In אֵין כֵּאלֹהֵינוּ, three prefixes are repeated. They are בְּ, כְּ, and לְ. Remember, because בּ and כּ are family members, the prefixes בְּ and כְּ have the same meaning. Circle the prefix in each of these words:

כֵּאלֹהֵינוּ   לַאדוֹנֵינוּ   כְּמוֹשִׁיעֵנוּ   לְמַלְכֵּנוּ   כַּאדוֹנֵינוּ

Write the meaning of each prefix. _____ כ, בְּ _____ ל

This hymn has one suffix that repeats over and over. Look for the repeating suffix in these words that describe God.

אֱלֹהֵינוּ means "our God."

אֲדוֹנֵינוּ means "our sovereign."

מַלְכֵּנוּ means "our ruler."

מוֹשִׁיעֵנוּ means "our savior."

Each of these words ends with the suffix _____.

This suffix means _____.

You know the beginning (prefix) and the ending (suffix) of each word below.

___   ___   ___   ___

כְּמוֹשִׁיעֵנוּ   כְּמַלְכֵּנוּ   לַאדוֹנֵינוּ   כֵּאלֹהֵינוּ

Write the number of the matching English meaning above each Hebrew word.

1. like our ruler   2. to our sovereign

3. like our savior   4. like our God

Now circle the main part *(not the prefix or suffix)* of each Hebrew word above. *(The first one has been done for you.)*

NAMES FOR GOD

Each of the main parts you circled on the previous page is actually a name for God. You may not recognize them at first, because when a word has prefix or suffix added, it may change its vowels or lose a final letter.

Connect the names for God in column 1 to the related words from אֵין כֵּאלֹהֵינוּ in column 2.

<table>
<tr><td align="center">2</td><td align="center">1</td><td></td></tr>
<tr><td align="center">אֱלֹהֵינוּ</td><td align="center">מֶלֶךְ</td><td>_____</td></tr>
<tr><td align="center">מַלְכֵּנוּ</td><td align="center">אָדוֹן</td><td>_____</td></tr>
<tr><td align="center">אֲדוֹנֵינוּ</td><td align="center">מוֹשִׁיעַ</td><td>_____</td></tr>
<tr><td align="center">מוֹשִׁיעֵנוּ</td><td align="center">אֱלֹהִים</td><td>_____</td></tr>
</table>

Now write the English meaning for the words in column 1 in the blank spaces.

A HYMN OF PRAISE

אֵין כֵּאלֹהֵינוּ was written before the ninth century C.E. It is over 1,000 years old! This hymn is an important statement of our belief in God.

Reread the English translation of אֵין כֵּאלֹהֵינוּ on page 90.

In your own words, describe the Jewish belief in God that is expressed in אֵין כֵּאלֹהֵינוּ.

_____

_____

 WHERE WE ARE

In many congregations אֵין כֵּאלֹהֵינוּ is sung before the עָלֵינוּ. Look ahead to page 94 to find when אֵין כֵּאלֹהֵינוּ is often sung in Reform congregations. On Shabbat morning, אֵין כֵּאלֹהֵינוּ might be sung before the עָלֵינוּ or after the_____.

אֵין כֵּאלֹהֵינוּ

Shabbat Morning Service

94

מִלּוֹן

א

fathers	אָבוֹת
our fathers	אֲבוֹתֵינוּ
our parent	אָבִינוּ
Abraham	אַבְרָהָם
our sovereign	אֲדוֹנֵינוּ
light	אוֹר
one	אֶחָד
(there) is none	אֵין
there is none like	אֵין כּ
eating (of)	אֲכִילַת
God of	אֱלֹהֵי
our God	אֱלֹהֵינוּ
mothers	אִמָהוֹת
our mothers	אִמּוֹתֵינוּ
Amen	אָמֵן
truth	אֱמֶת
who	אֲשֶׁר
you (are)	אַתָּה
you are	אַתָּה הוּא

ב

in (with) love	בְּאַהֲבָה
among the gods (other nations worship)	בָּאֱלִם
in truth	בֶּאֱמֶת
who creates	בּוֹרֵא
at this season, at this time	בַּזְּמַן הַזֶּה
chose (choosing)	בָּחַר
we trust(ed)	בָּטַחְנוּ
on that day	בַּיּוֹם הַהוּא
your house	בֵּיתֶךָ
with God's commandments	בְּמִצְוֹתָיו
prophets	(בְּ)נְבִיאִים
us	בָּנוּ
people of	בְּנֵי
in the sukkah	בַּסֻּכָּה
in your eyes	בְּעֵינֶיךָ
in the world	בְּעָלְמָא
in (the) holiness	בְּקֹדֶשׁ
in God's holiness	בִּקְדֻשָׁתוֹ

and say	וְאִמְרוּ
and we	וַאֲנַחְנוּ
and creates	וּבוֹרֵא
and in the life of	וּבְחַיֵּי
and in (with) favor	וּבְרָצוֹן
and the word of	וּדְבַר
and the awesome	וְהַנּוֹרָא
and this is	וְזֹאת
and life (of)	וְחַיֵּי
and may it be good	וְטוֹב
and will rule	וְיַמְלִיךְ
and will be praised	וְיִשְׁתַּבַּח
and will be holy	וְיִתְקַדַּשׁ
and shield	וּמָגֵן
and thank	וּמוֹדִים
and rescuer	וּמוֹשִׁיעַ
and your reign	וּמֶמְשַׁלְתְּךָ
and gave (and giving)	וְנָתַן
and for, and on	וְעַל
and righteousness (justice)	וָצֶדֶק
and commands us	וְצִוָּנוּ
and eternal	וְקַיָּם

ז

memory	זֵכֶר
memory	זִכָּרוֹן

ח

living, lives	חַי
(of) life, the living	חַיִּים
graciousness	חֵן
Hanukkah	חֲנֻכָּה
acts of loving-kindness	חֲסָדִים טוֹבִים
darkness	חֹשֶׁךְ

ט

goodness	טוֹבָה
good (faithful)	טוֹבִים

blessed, praised	בָּרוּךְ
with compassion, mercy	בְּרַחֲמִים
blessed	בְּרִיךְ
praise!	בָּרְכוּ
blessing	בִּרְכָתָא
with your peace	בִּשְׁלוֹמֶךָ

ג

mighty, powerful	גִּבּוֹר
your greatness	גָּדְלֶךָ
acts of loving-kindness	גְמִילוּת חֲסָדִים

ד

things	דְּבָרִים
ways of	דַּרְכֵי
its ways	דְּרָכֶיהָ

ה

the earth	הָאֲדָמָה
the earth, the land	הָאָרֶץ
the one who chooses	הַבּוֹחֵר
the mighty	הַגִּבּוֹר
the great	הַגָּדוֹל
the vine	הַגֶּפֶן
the words	הַדְּבָרִים
all things, everything, of all	הַכֹּל
who is to be praised	הַמְבֹרָךְ
who brings forth	הַמּוֹצִיא
spoken	הַנֶּאֱמָרִים
the worship	הָעֲבוֹדָה
the world	הָעוֹלָם
the nations	הָעַמִּים
merciful, the mercy	הָרַחֲמִים
the Torah	הַתּוֹרָה

ע

you shall love	וְאָהַבְתָּ
and a love of kindness	וְאַהֲבַת חֶסֶד

95

י

will be	יִהְיֶה
forms	יוֹצֵר
Adonai	יְיָ
will rule	יִמְלֹךְ
Jacob	יַעֲקֹב
(will) make	יַעֲשֶׂה
Isaac	יִצְחָק
Jerusalem	יְרוּשָׁלַיִם
Israel	יִשְׂרָאֵל
will be great	יִתְגַּדַּל

כ

glory of	כְּבוֹד
God's glory	כְּבוֹדוֹ
all	כָּל
all of us as one	כֻּלָּנוּ כְּאֶחָד
like you	כָּמוֹךָ
like you	כָּמֹכָה, כָּמְכָה
(like) your deeds	(כְּ)מַעֲשֶׂיךָ

ל

God	(לַ)אֲדוֹן
Leah	לֵאָה
as a sign	לְאוֹת
your heart	לְבָבְךָ
to bless	לְבָרֵךְ
from generation to generation	לְדוֹר וָדוֹר
to light	לְהַדְלִיק
to save	לְהוֹשִׁיעַ
lulav	לוּלָב
bread	לֶחֶם
going out from from Egypt	(לְ)יִצִיאַת מִצְרַיִם
work of creation	(לְ)מַעֲשֶׂה בְרֵאשִׁית
to us	לָנוּ
eternally	לְעוֹלָם
forever and ever	לְעוֹלָם וָעֶד
forever	לְעָלַם
to God's people	לְעַמּוֹ
before	לִפְנֵי
to praise	לְשַׁבֵּחַ

מ

happy	מְאַשֵּׁר
our savior	מוֹשִׁיעֵנוּ
mezuzot, doorposts	מְזֻזוֹת
gives life	מְחַיֶּה
who	מִי
who is like	מִי כ
who is like you?	מִי כָמוֹךָ
from Jerusalem	מִירוּשָׁלַיִם
from all	מִכָּל
(is) ruler	מֶלֶךְ
Ruler of rulers	מֶלֶךְ מַלְכֵי הַמְּלָכִים
ruled	מָלַךְ
God's kingdom	מַלְכוּתֶהּ
God's kingdom	מַלְכוּתוֹ
your sovereignty	מַלְכוּתְךָ
our ruler	מַלְכֵּנוּ
from	מִן
brings on the evening	מַעֲרִיב עֲרָבִים
matzah	מַצָּה
from Zion	מִצִּיוֹן
maror, bitter herbs	מָרוֹר
Moses	מֹשֶׁה

נ

majestic	נֶאְדָּר
we will tell	נַגִּיד
we will give thanks to	נוֹדֶה ל
gives	נוֹתֵן
miracles	נִסִּים
pleasantness	נֹעַם
let us sanctify	נְקַדֵּשׁ
light, candle	נֵר
you gave	נָתַתָּ

ע

God's servant	עַבְדּוֹ
helper	עוֹזֵר
eternal, world	עוֹלָם
stands	עוֹמֵד
on	עַל
supreme	עֶלְיוֹן
for us, on us, it is our duty	עָלֵינוּ
God's people	עַמּוֹ
your people	עַמְּךָ
tree	עֵץ
makes	עֹשֶׂה

פ

(the) fruit (of)	פְּרִי

ק

sanctification	קִדּוּשׁ
holy	קַדִּישׁ
makes us holy	קִדְּשָׁנוּ

ר

great	רַב
Rebecca	רִבְקָה
Rachel	רָחֵל

ש

Shabbat	שַׁבָּת
who has given us life	שֶׁהֶחֱיָנוּ
shofar	שׁוֹפָר
grant, put	שִׂים
of	שֶׁל
peace	שָׁלוֹם
peace	שְׁלָמָא
three	שְׁלֹשָׁה
name	שֵׁם
placed, put	שָׂם
God's name	שְׁמֵהּ
your name	שִׁמְךָ
hear	שְׁמַע
who gave	שֶׁנָּתַן
Sarah	שָׂרָה

ת

Torah, teaching	תּוֹרָה
Torah of life	תּוֹרַת חַיִּים
Torah of	תּוֹרַת
God's Torah	תּוֹרָתוֹ